LANDSCAPES COLORING BOOK

Thanks for purchase this book!

If you enjoy it, please consider leave a review.

Lets color!

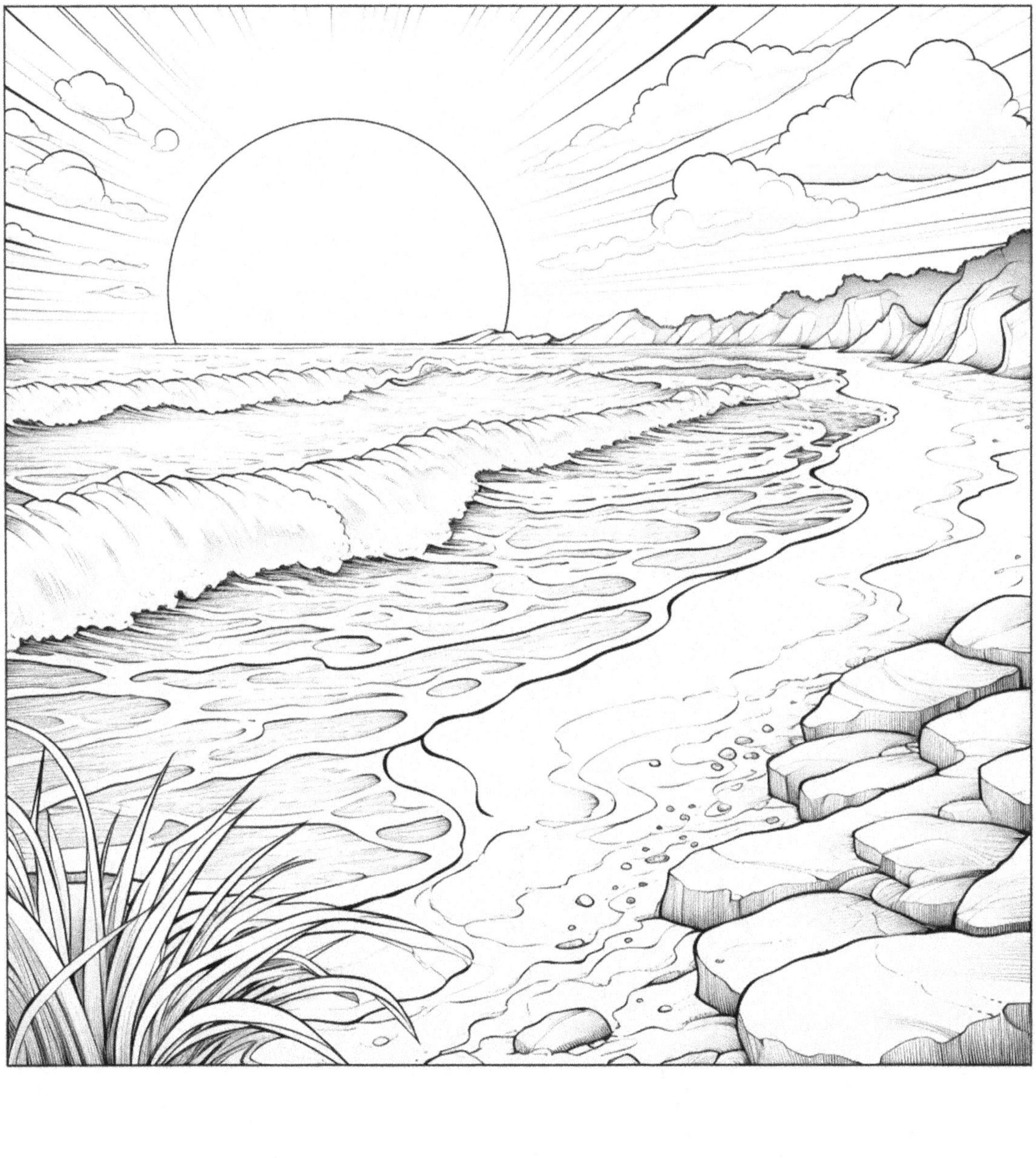

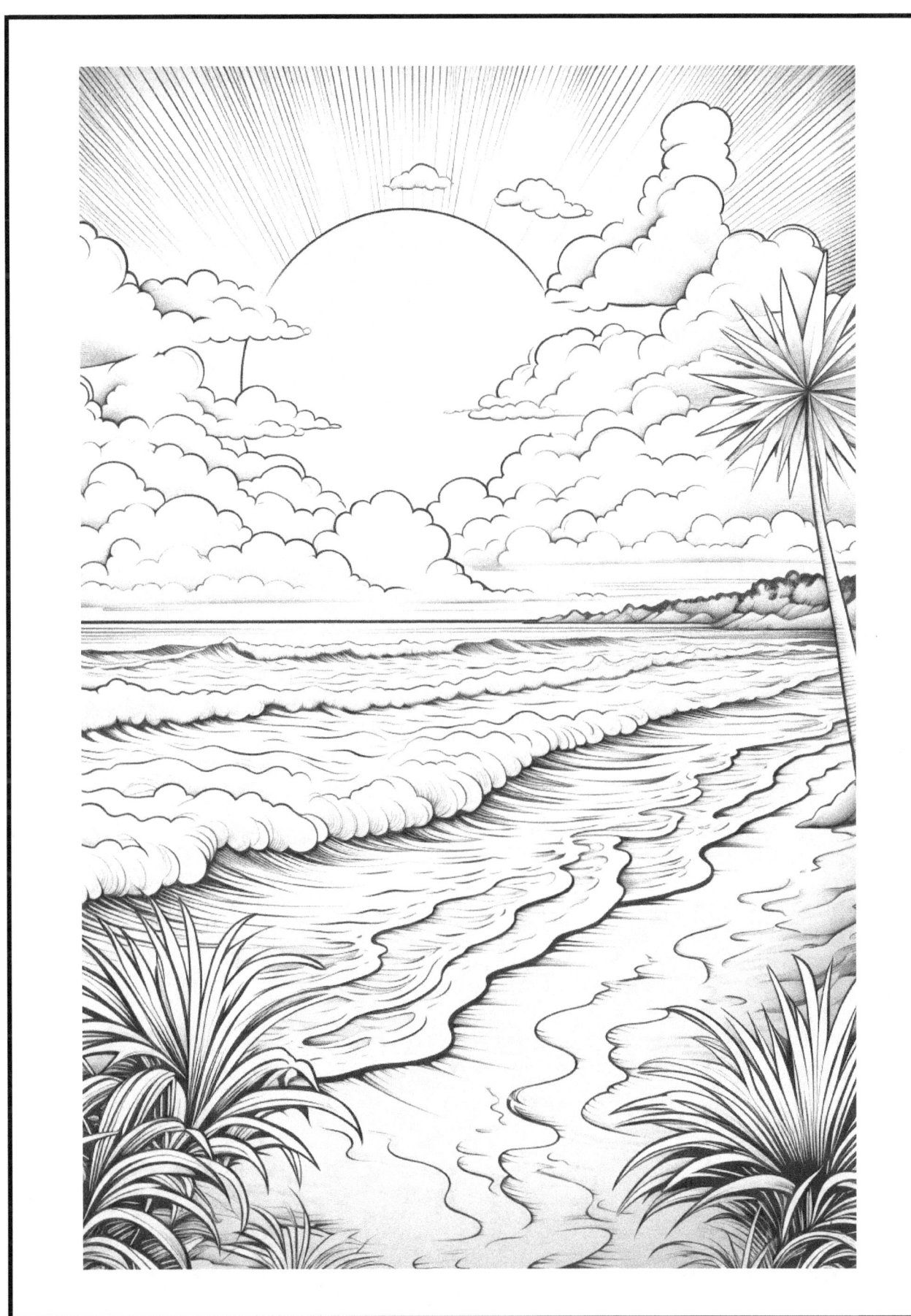

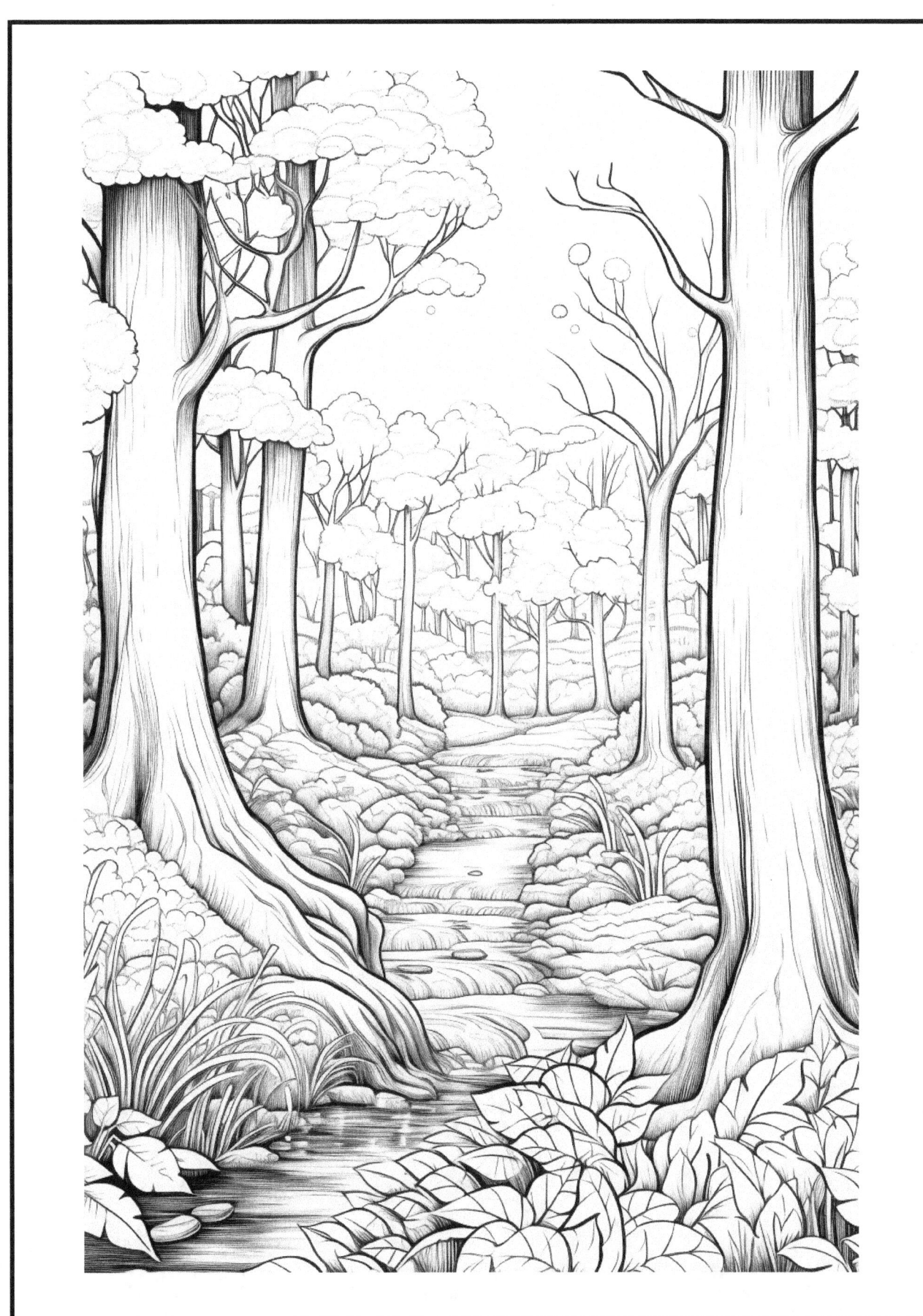

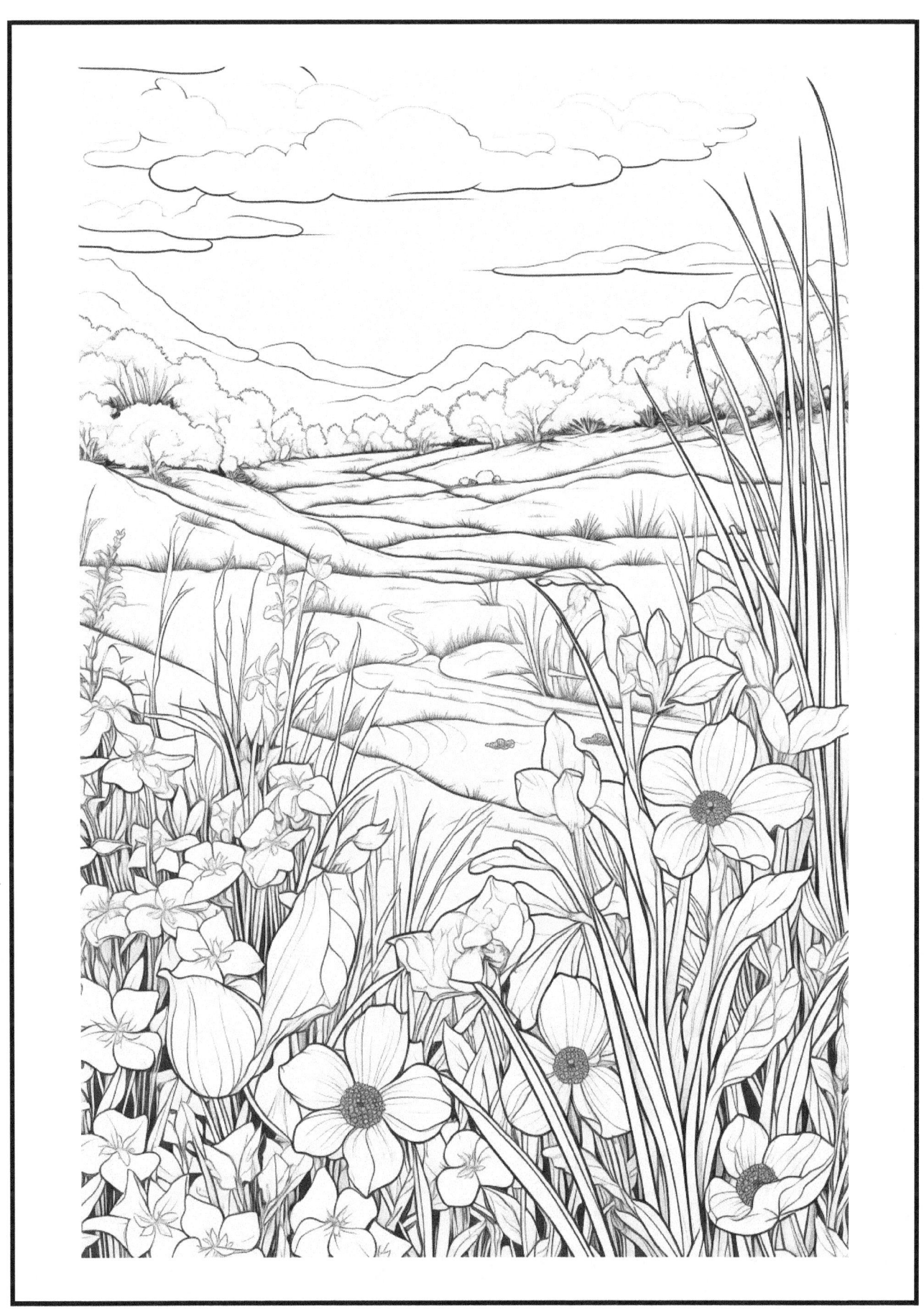

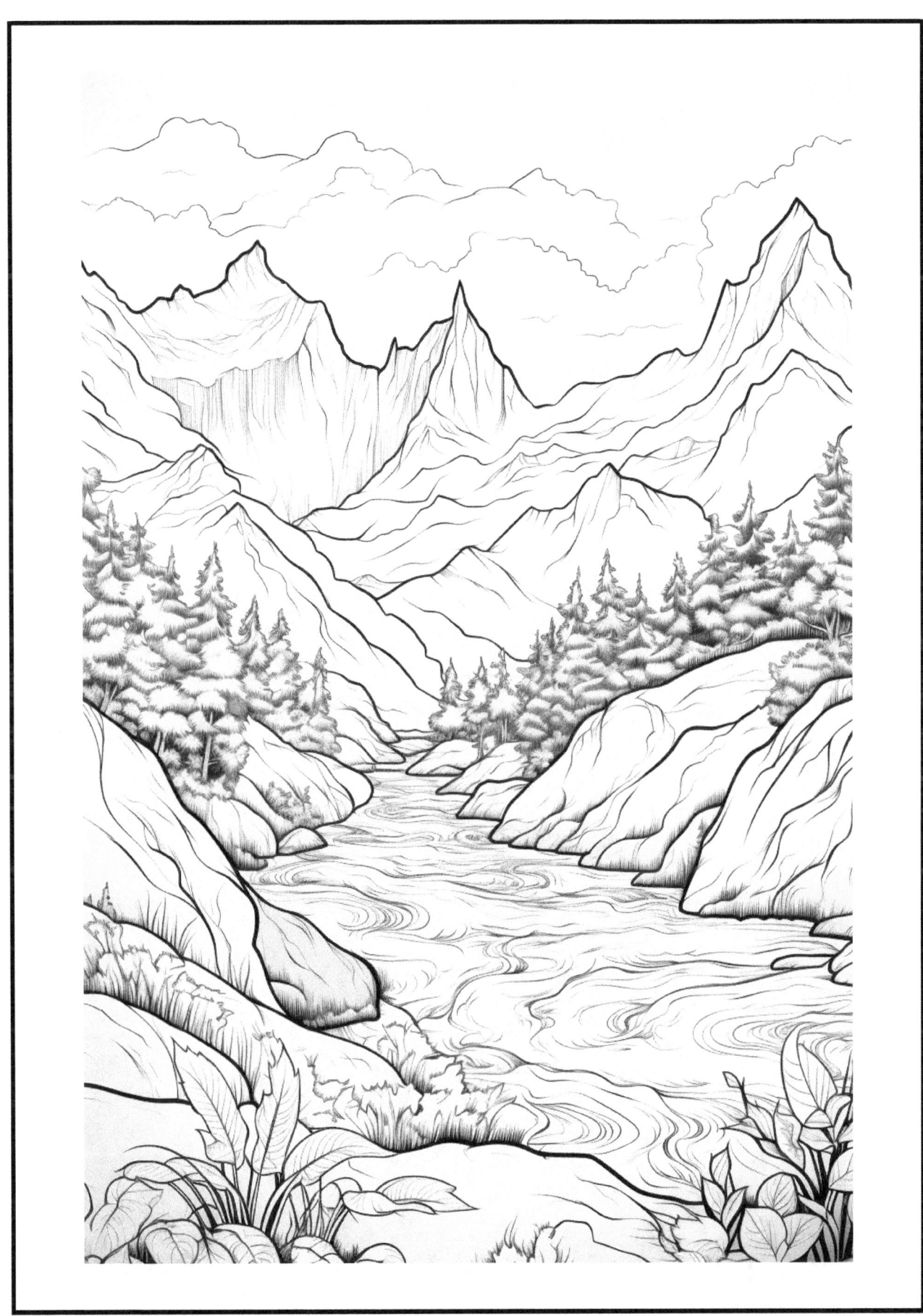

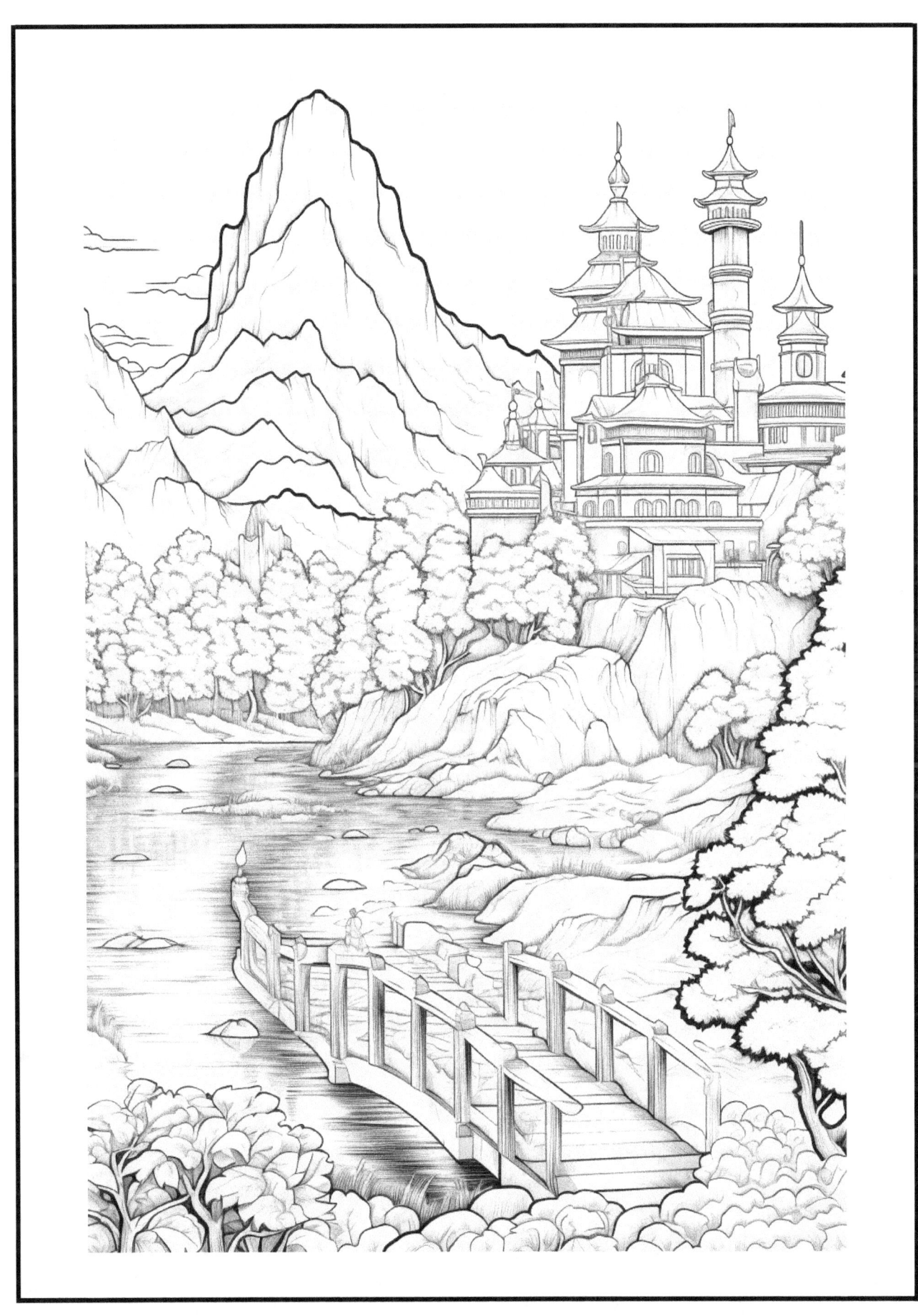

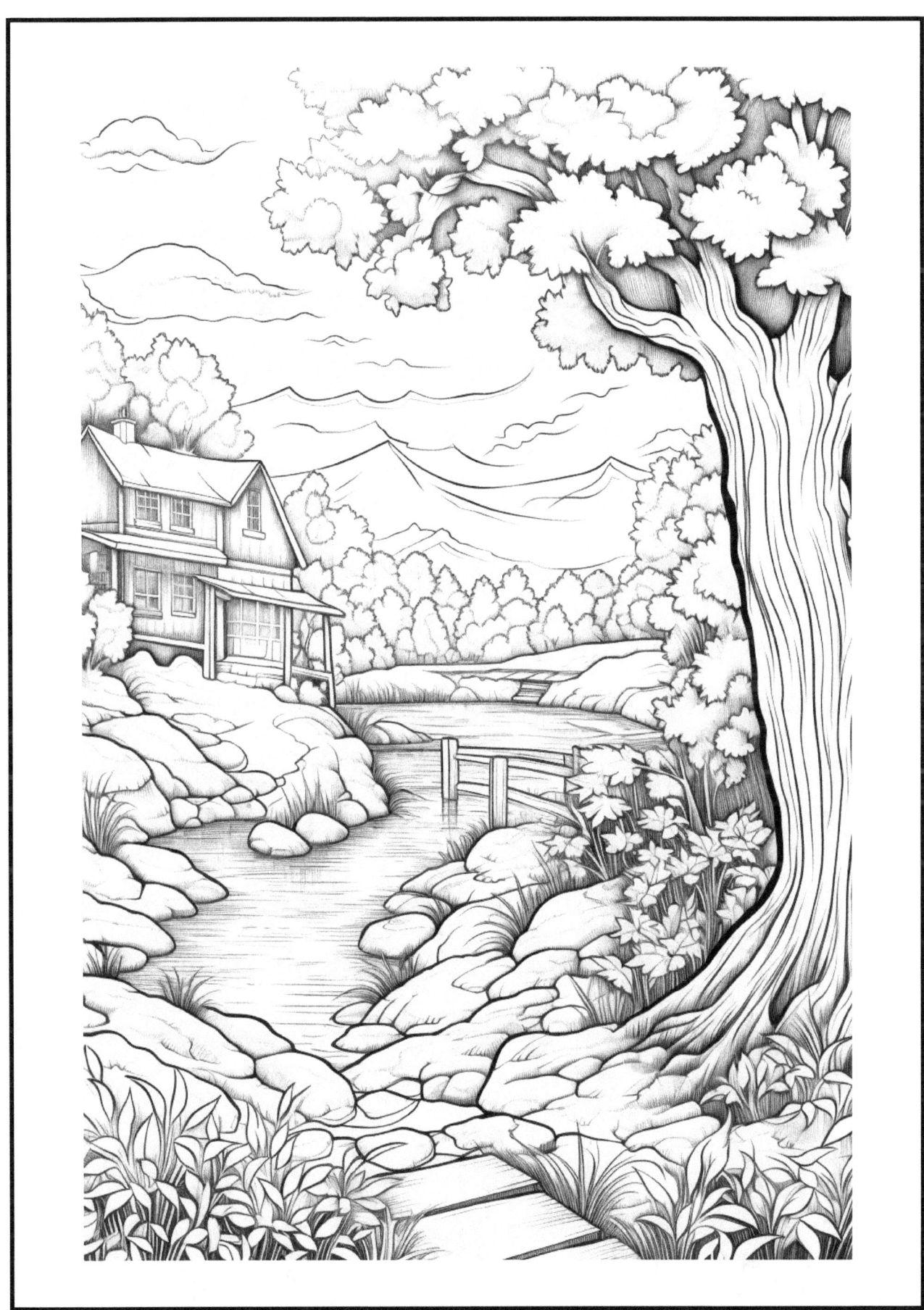

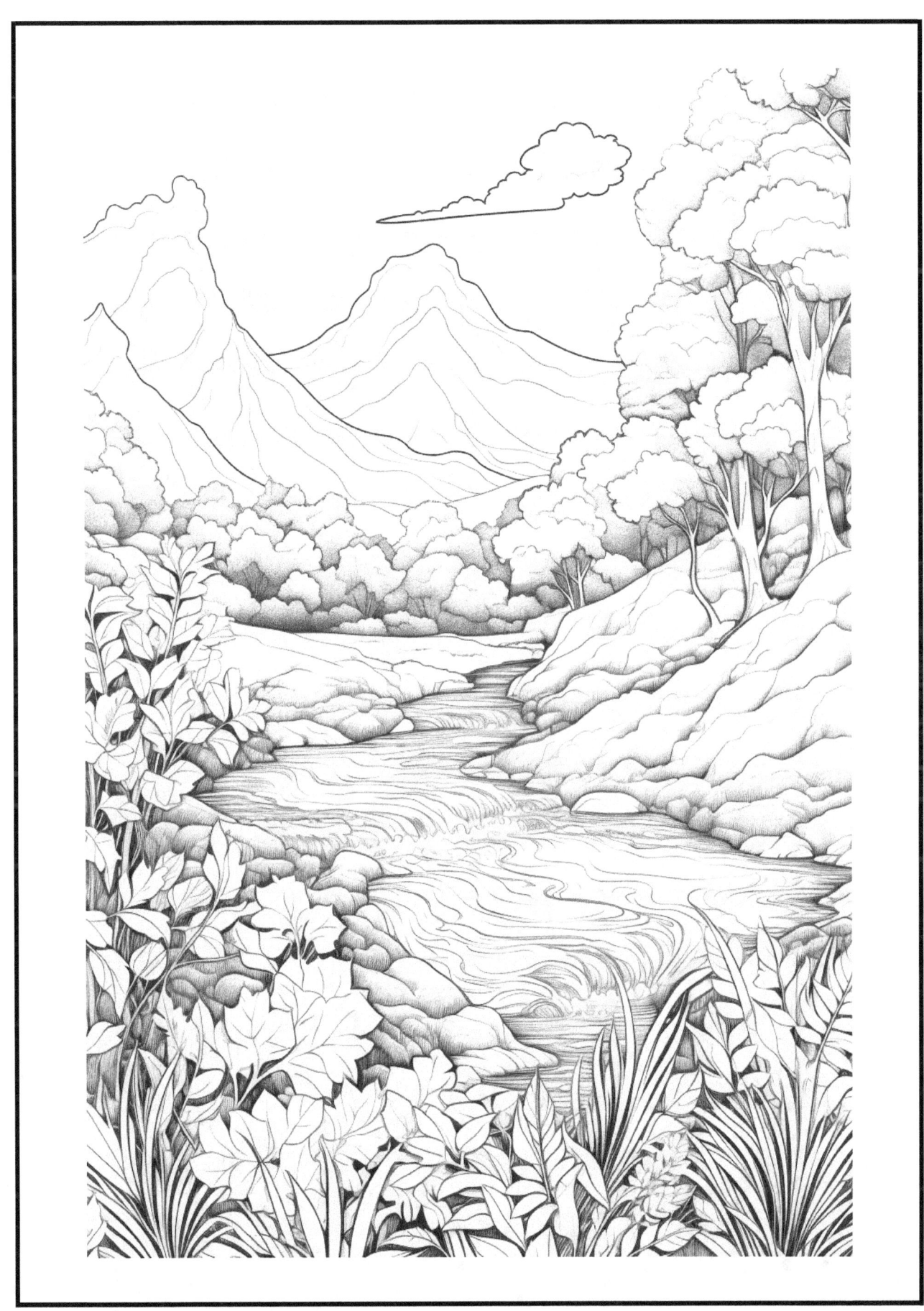

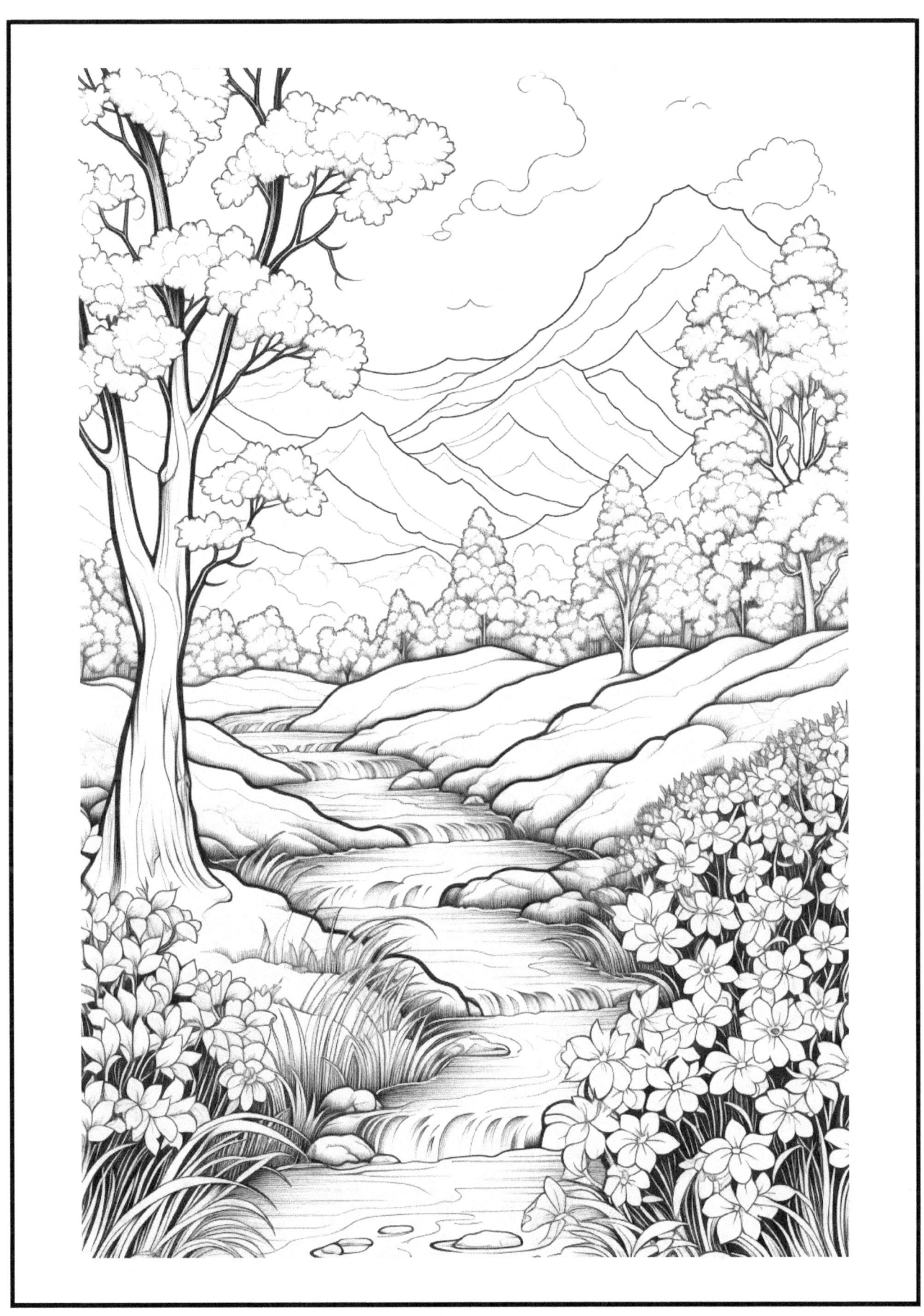

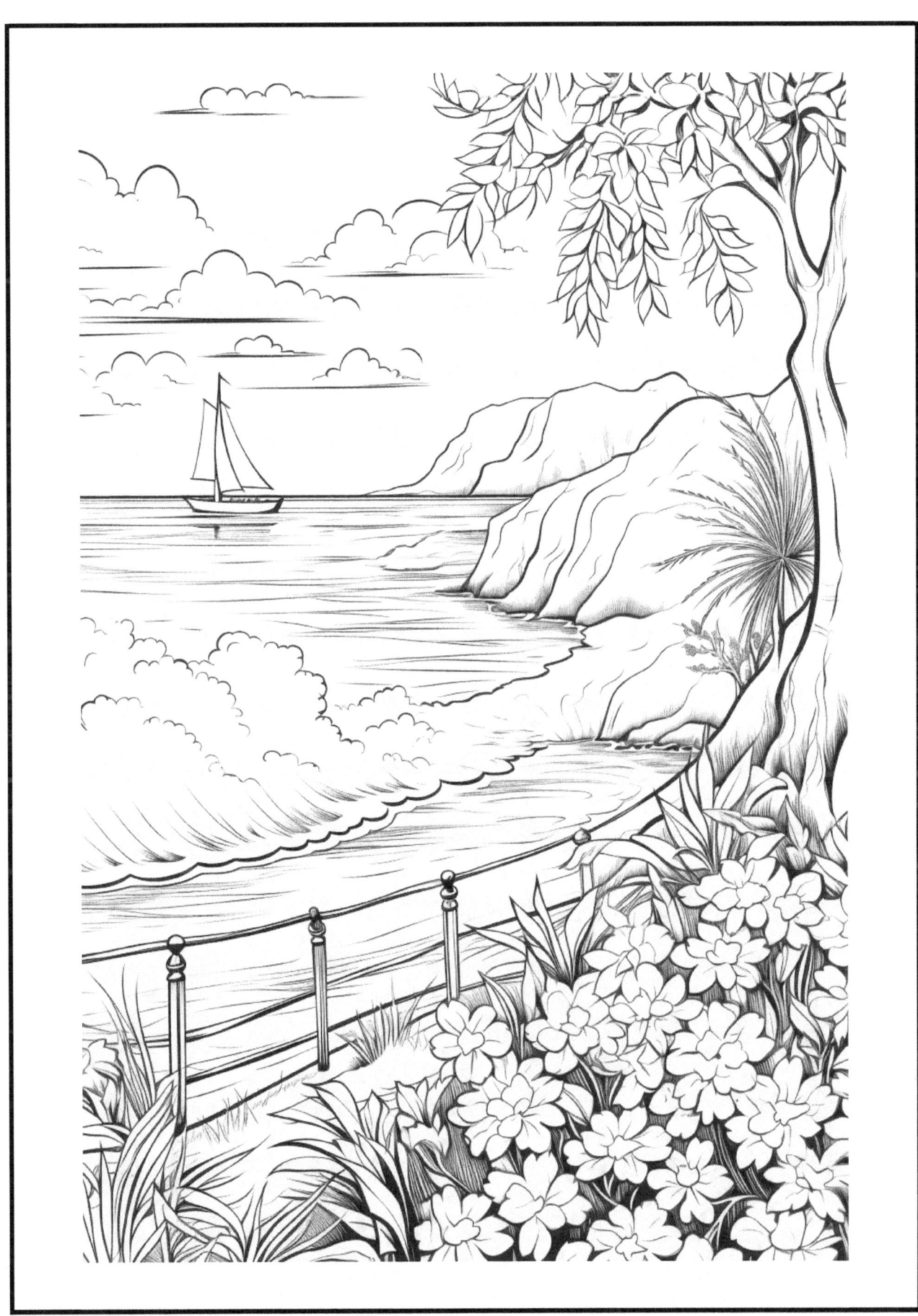

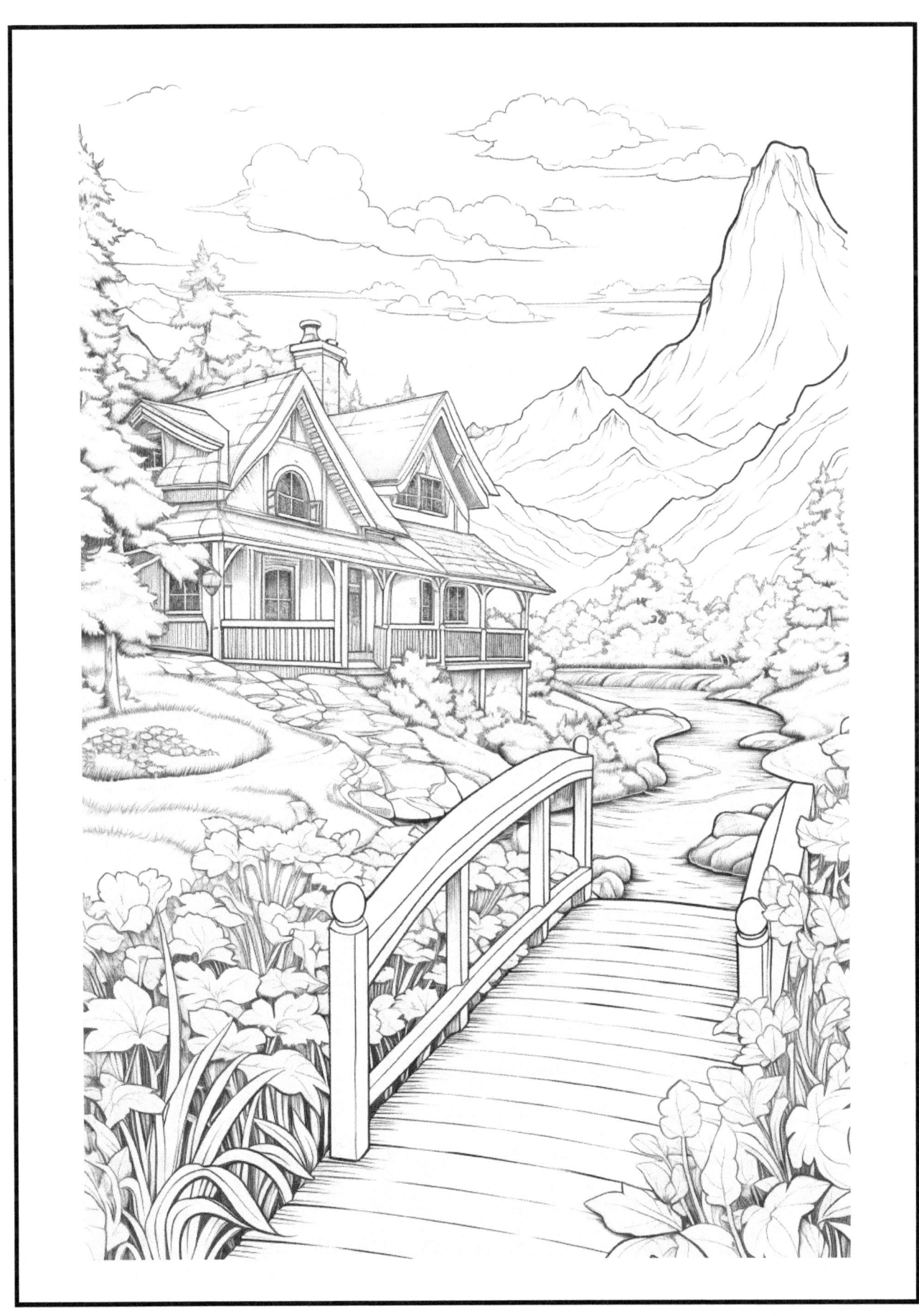

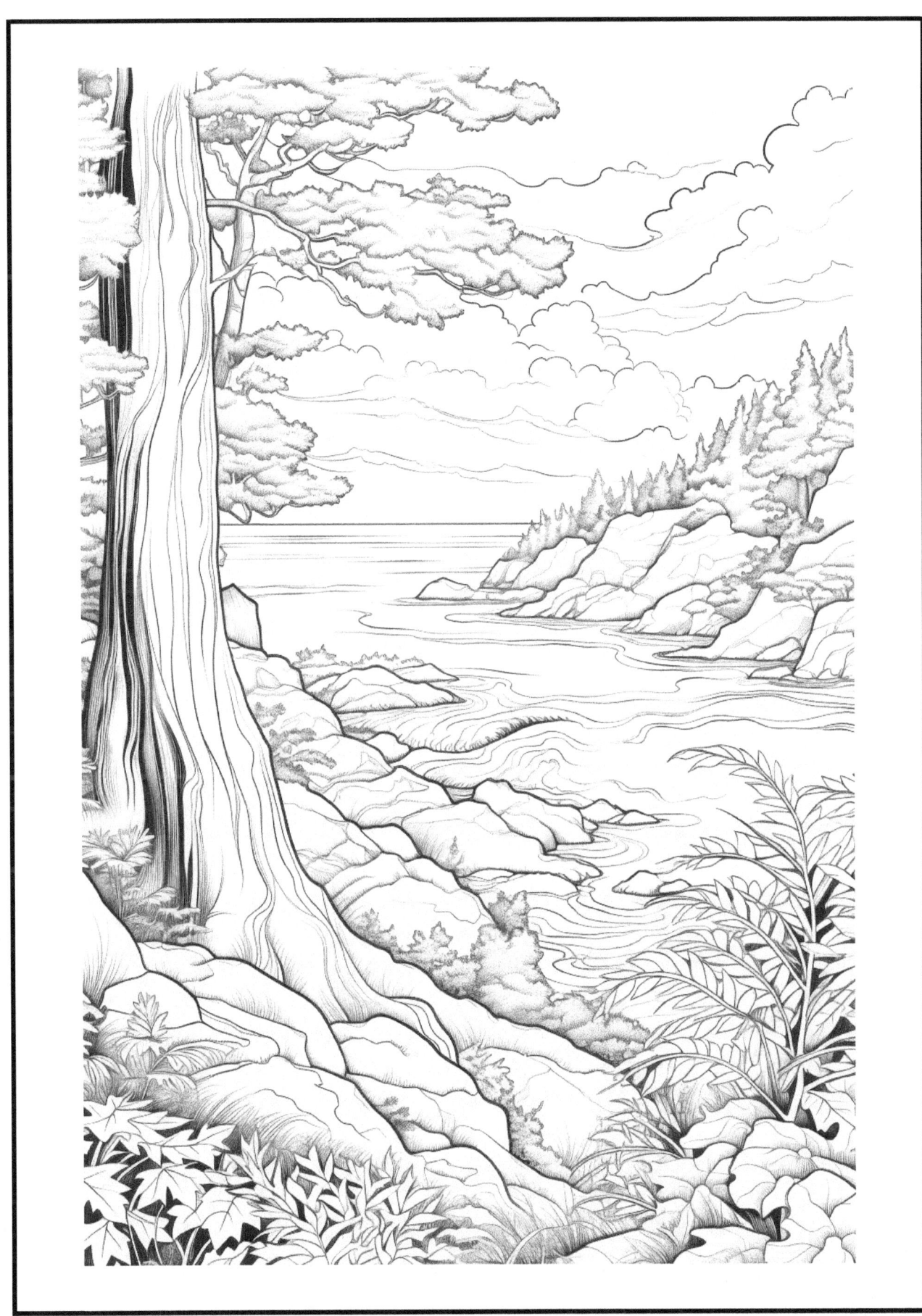

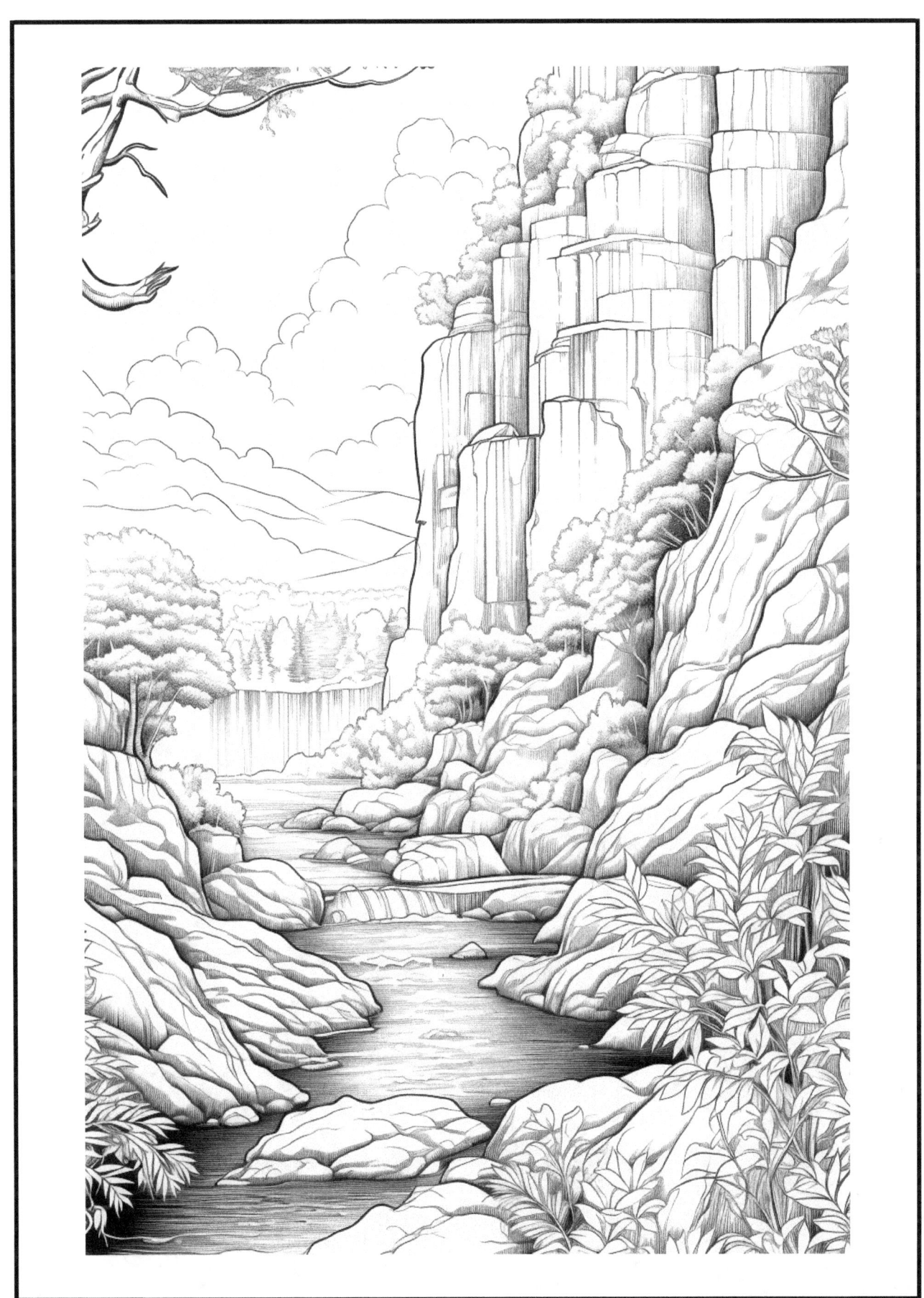

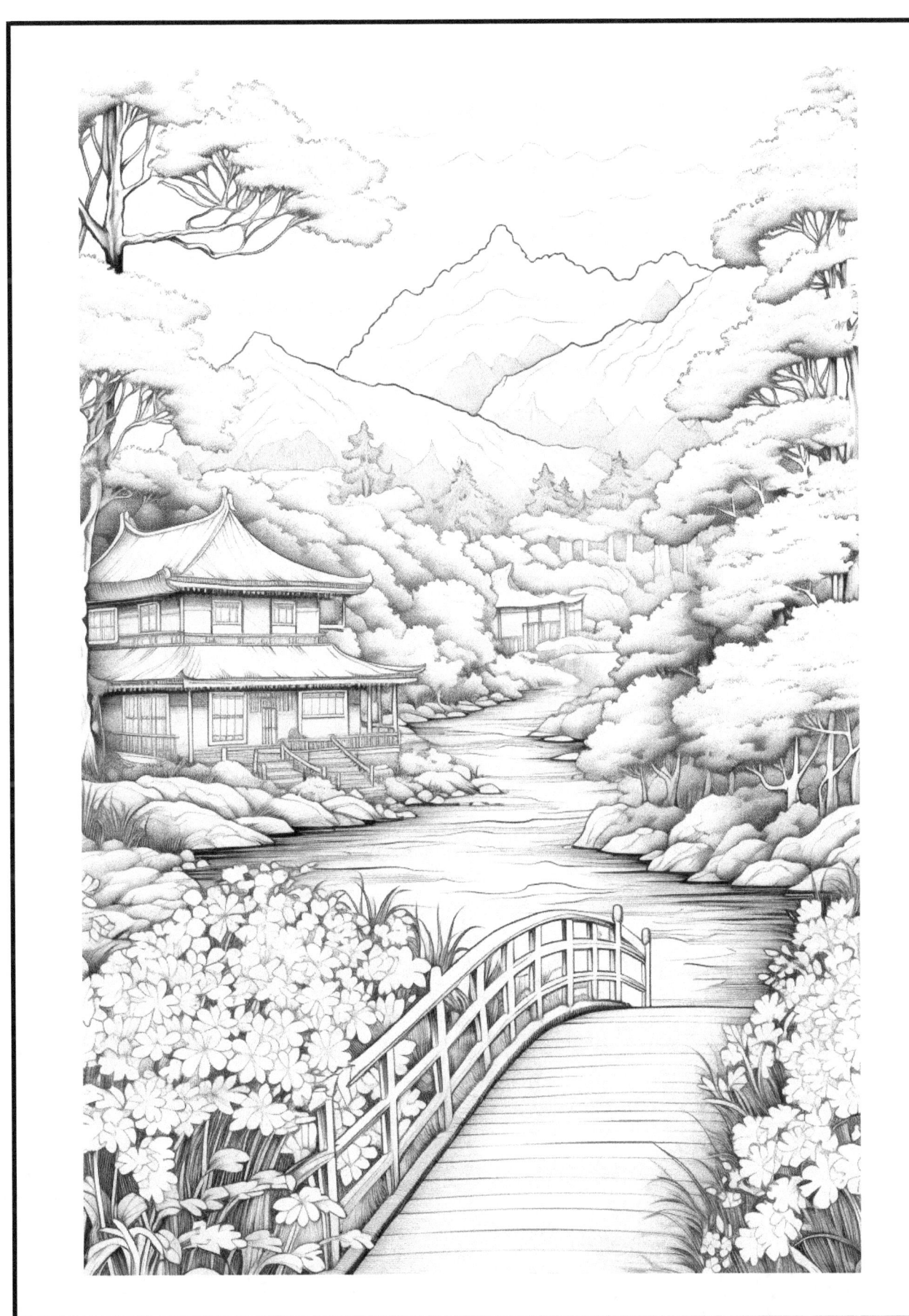

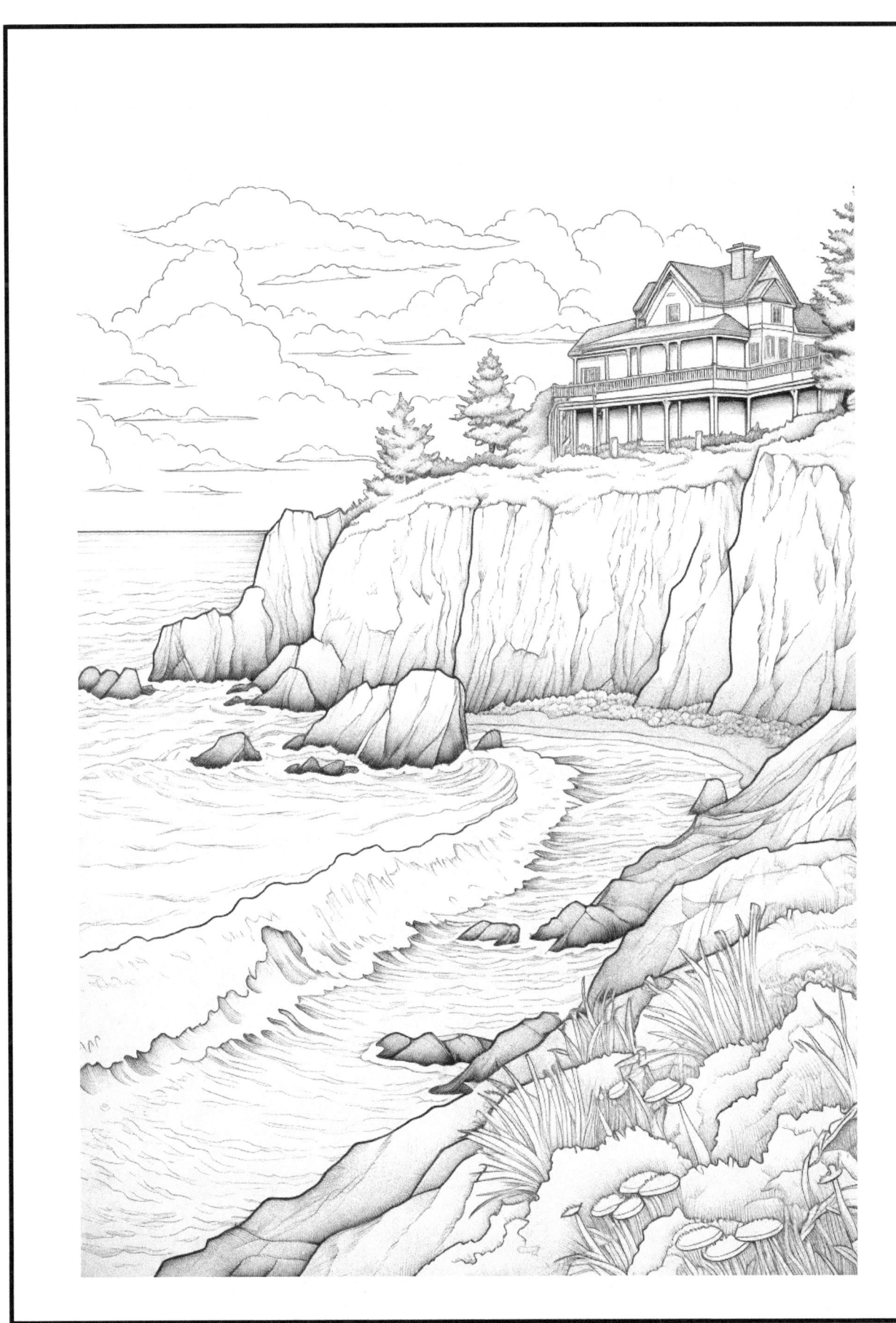

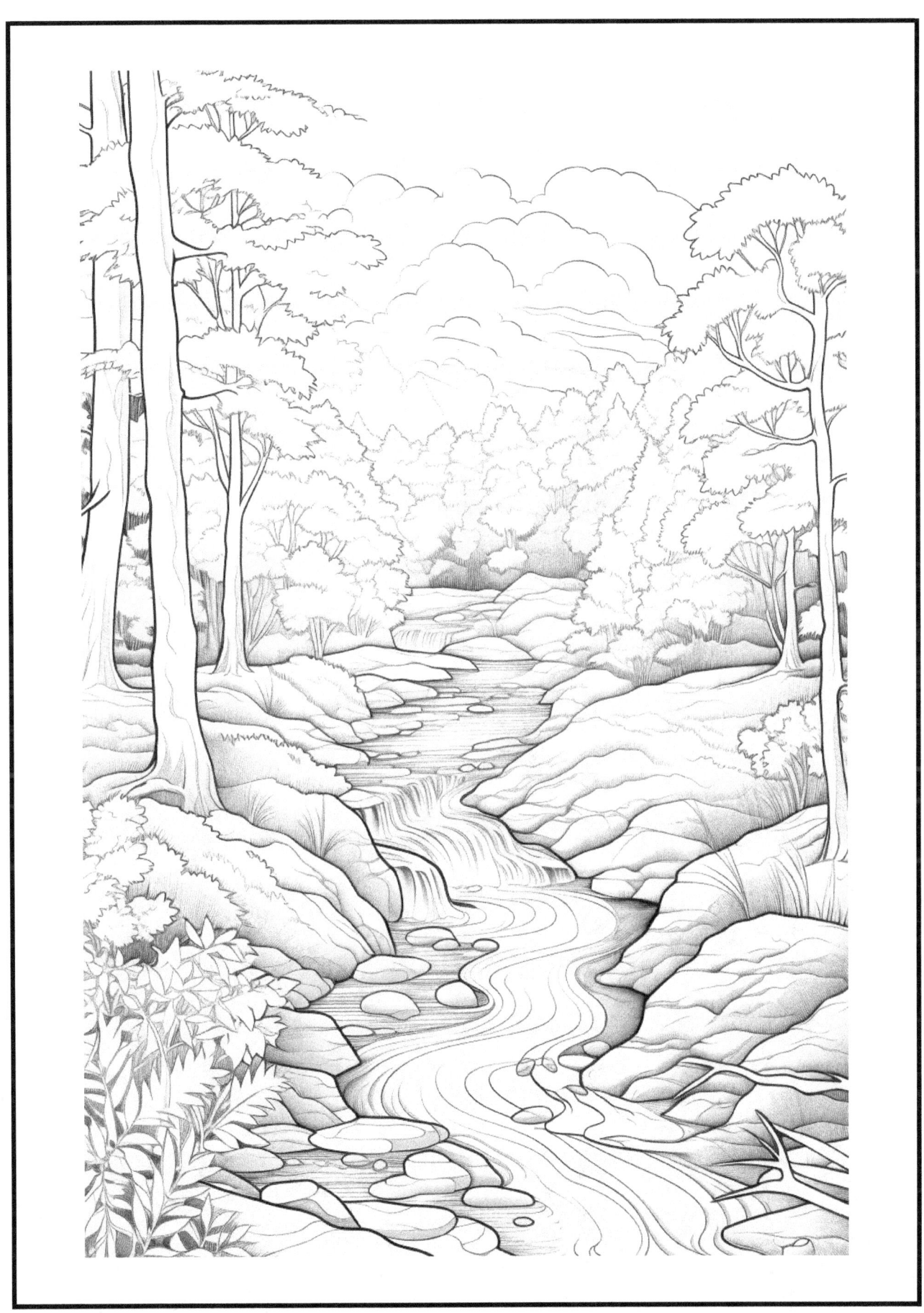

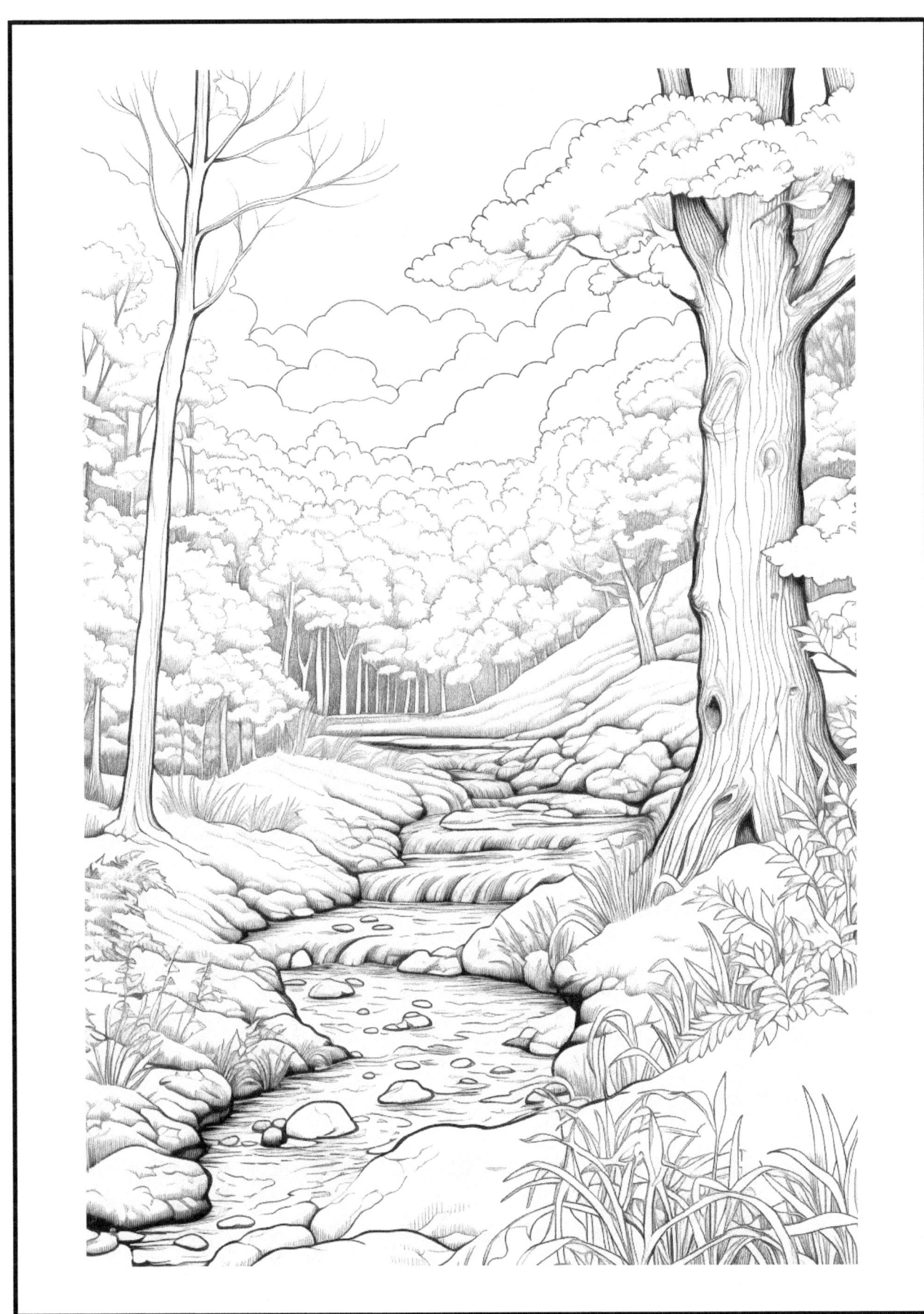

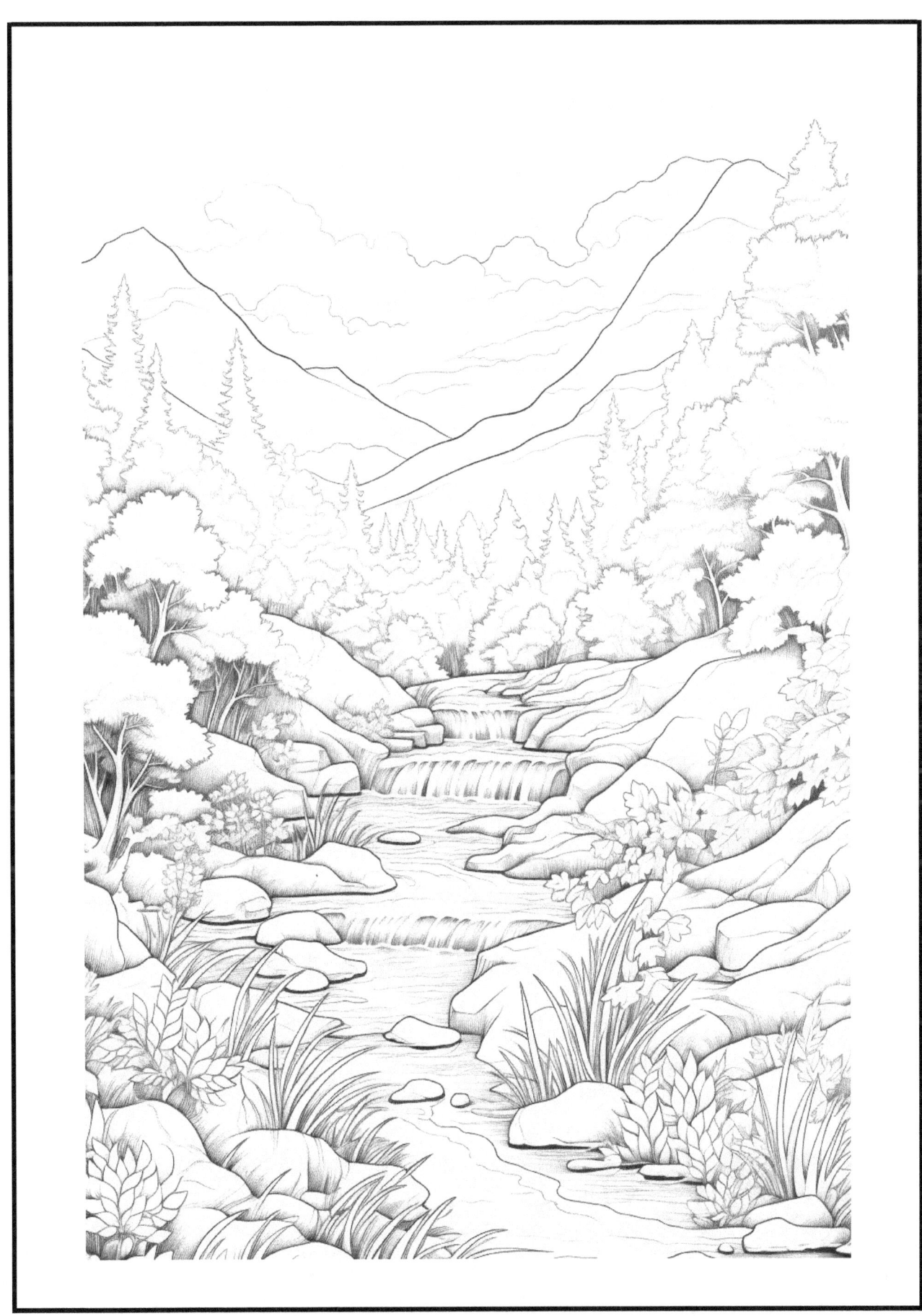

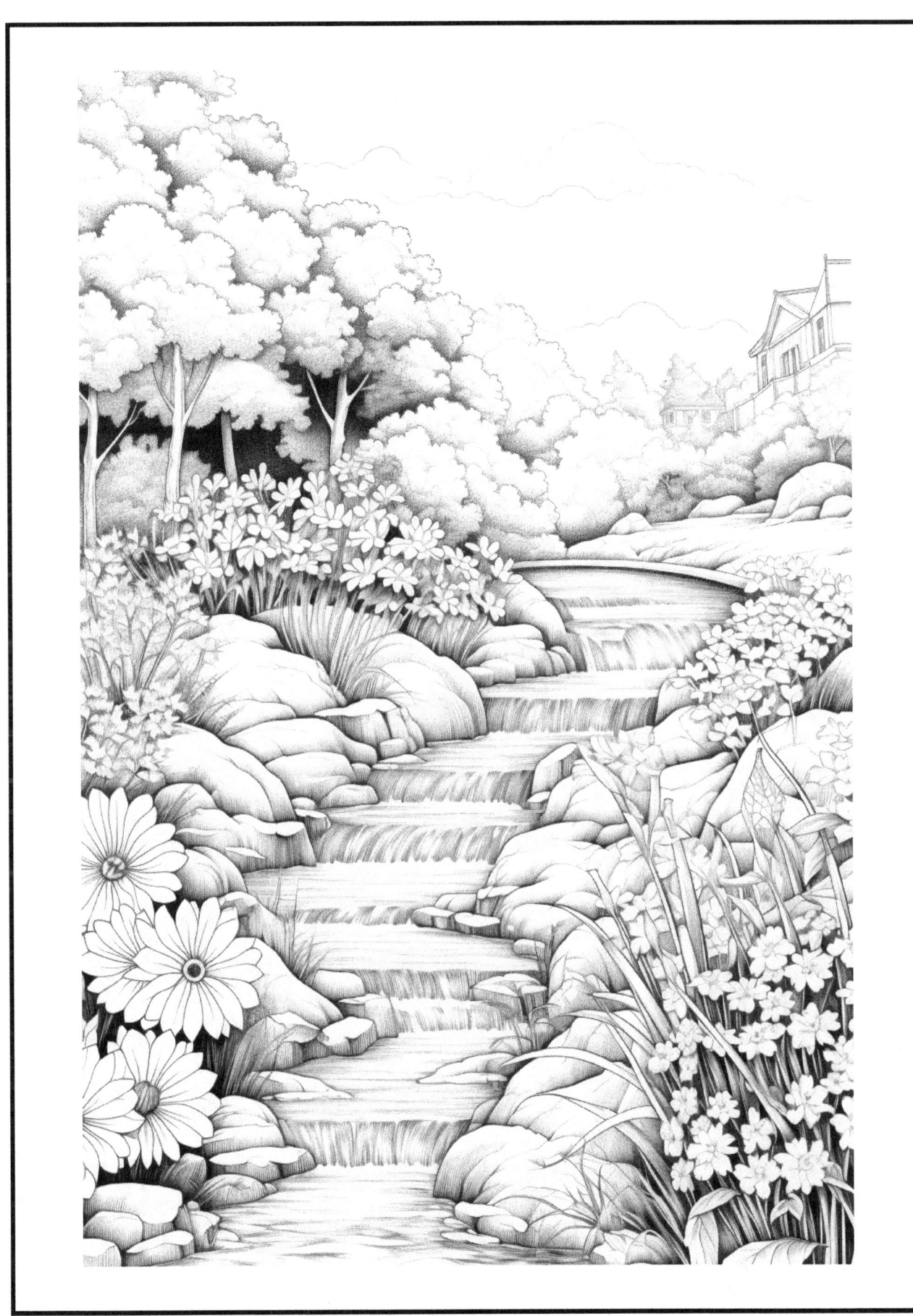

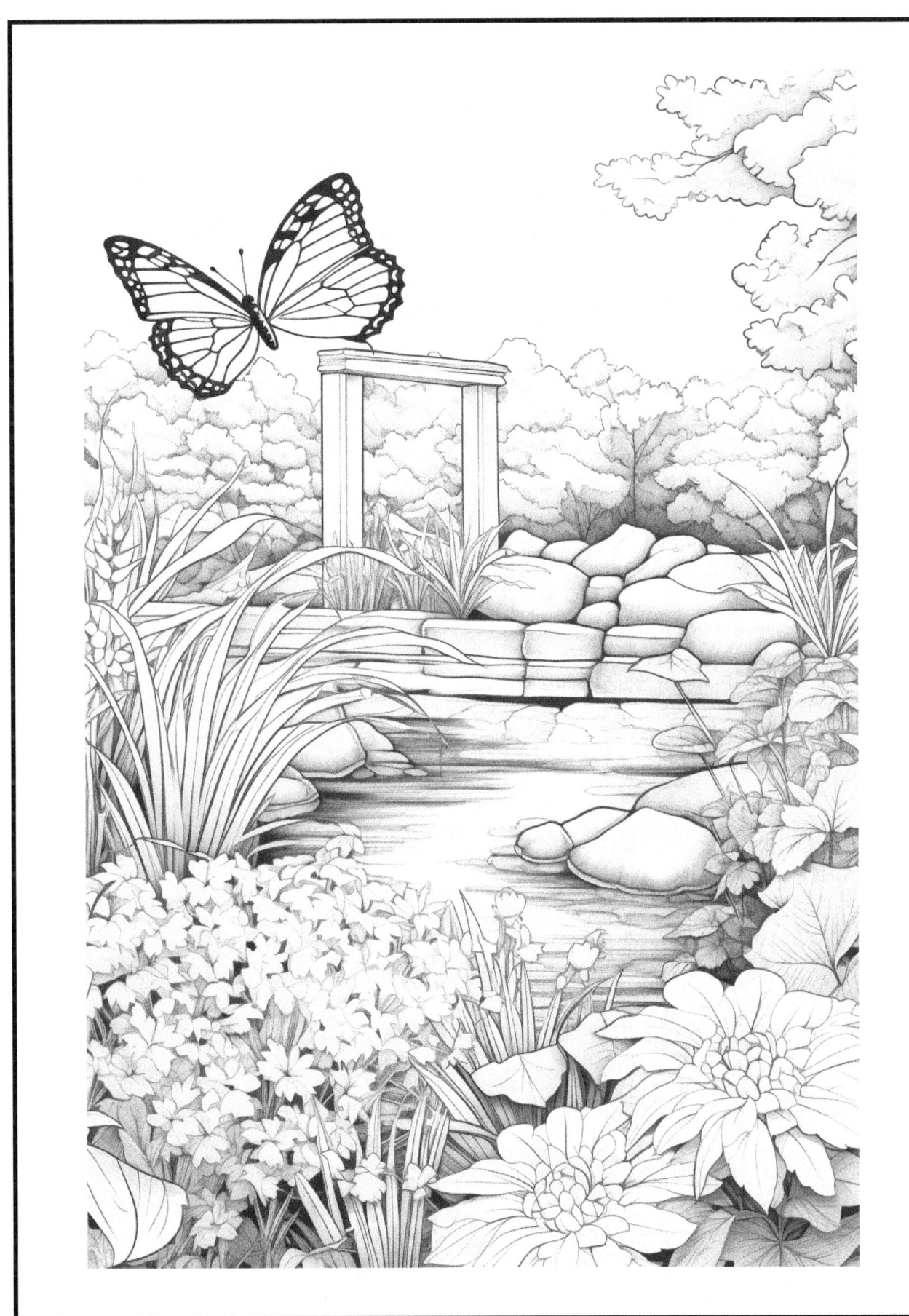

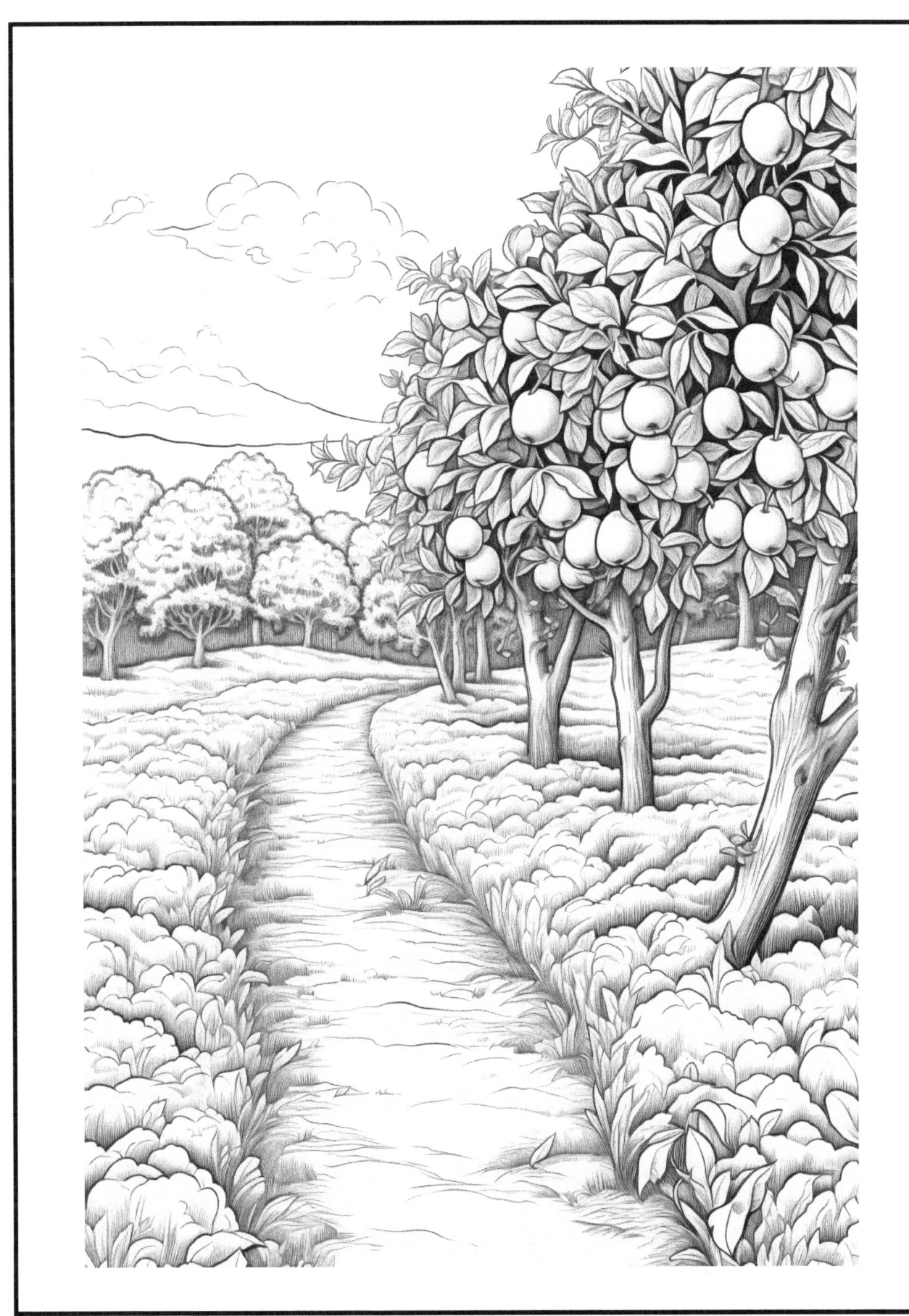

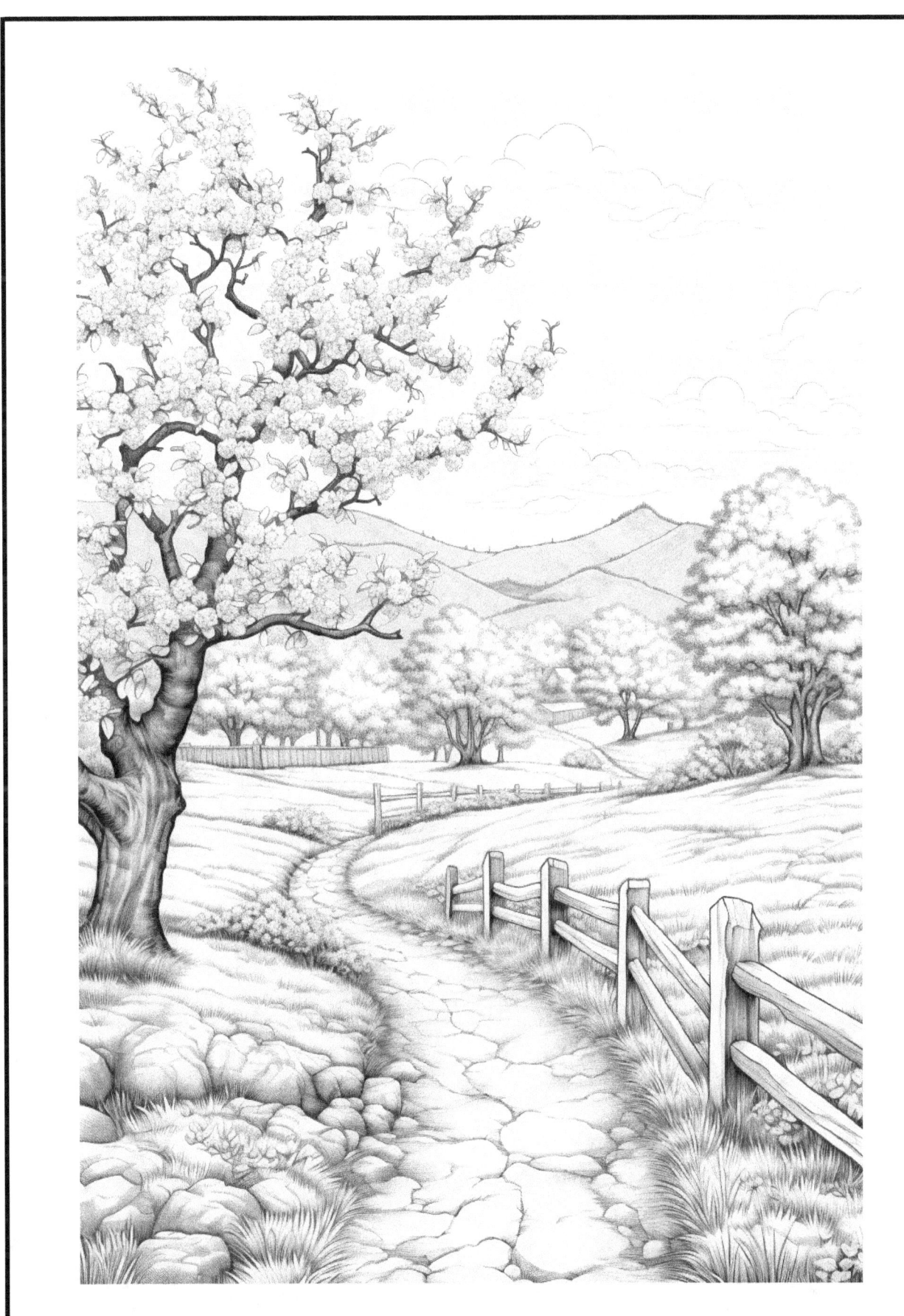

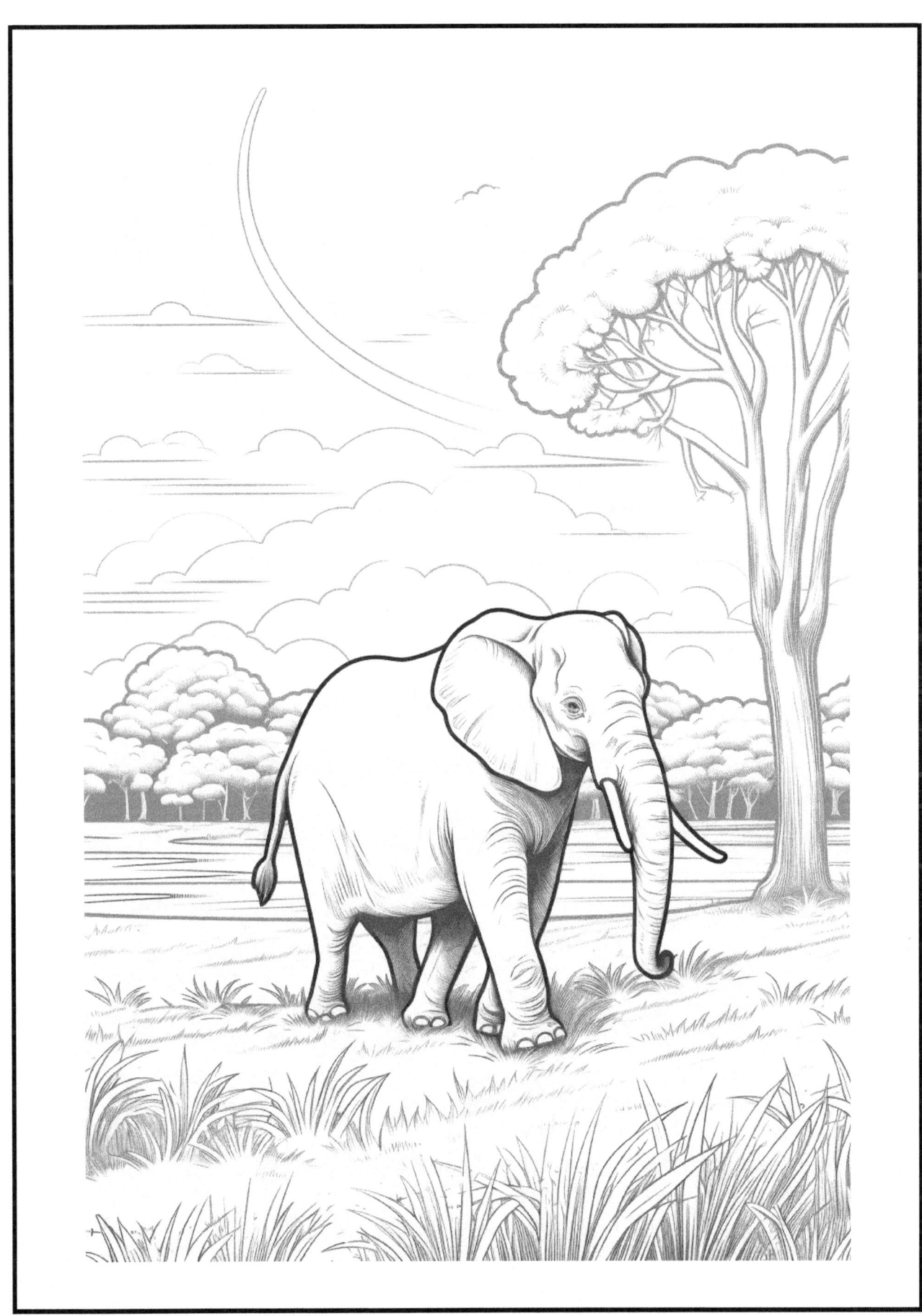

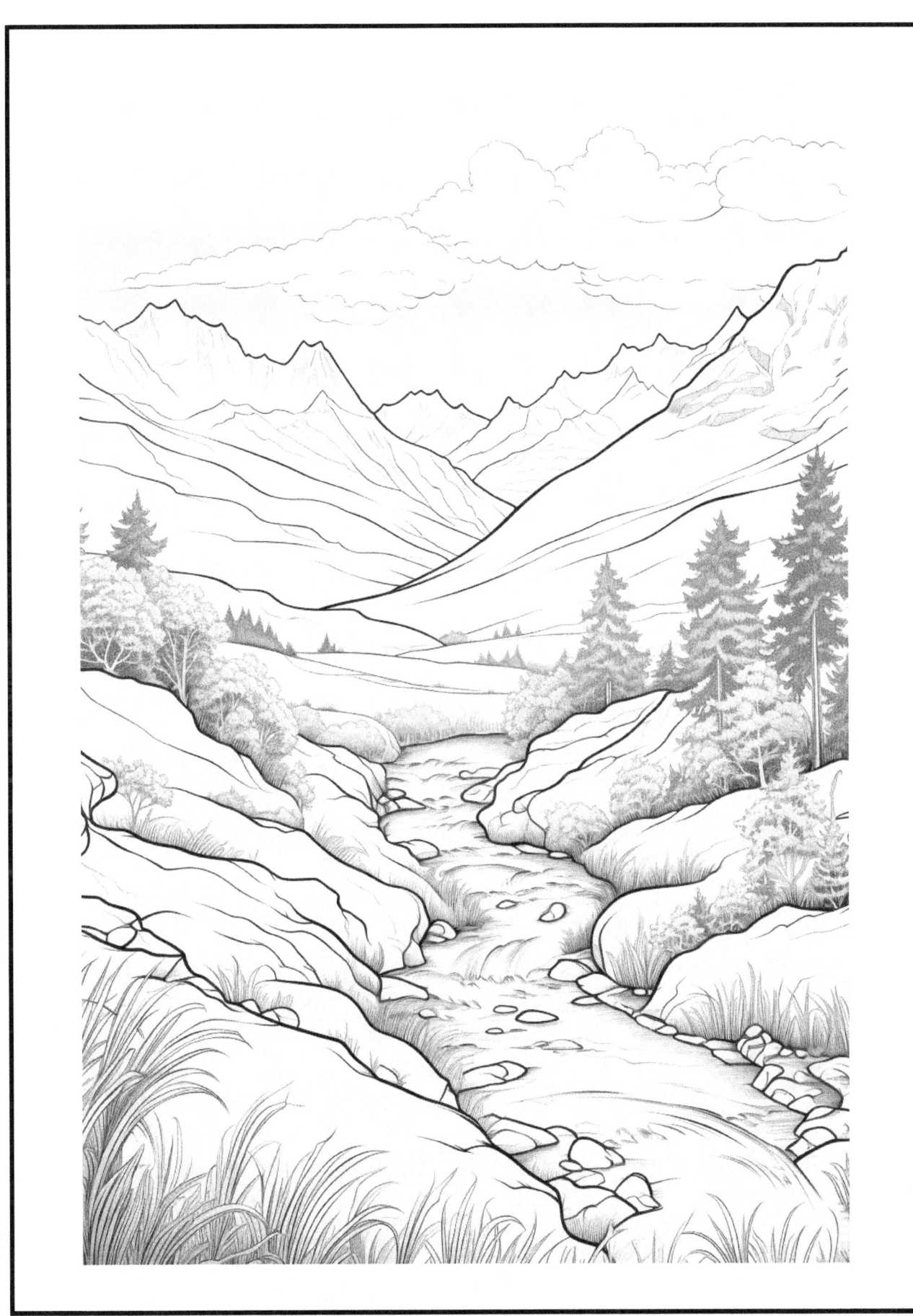

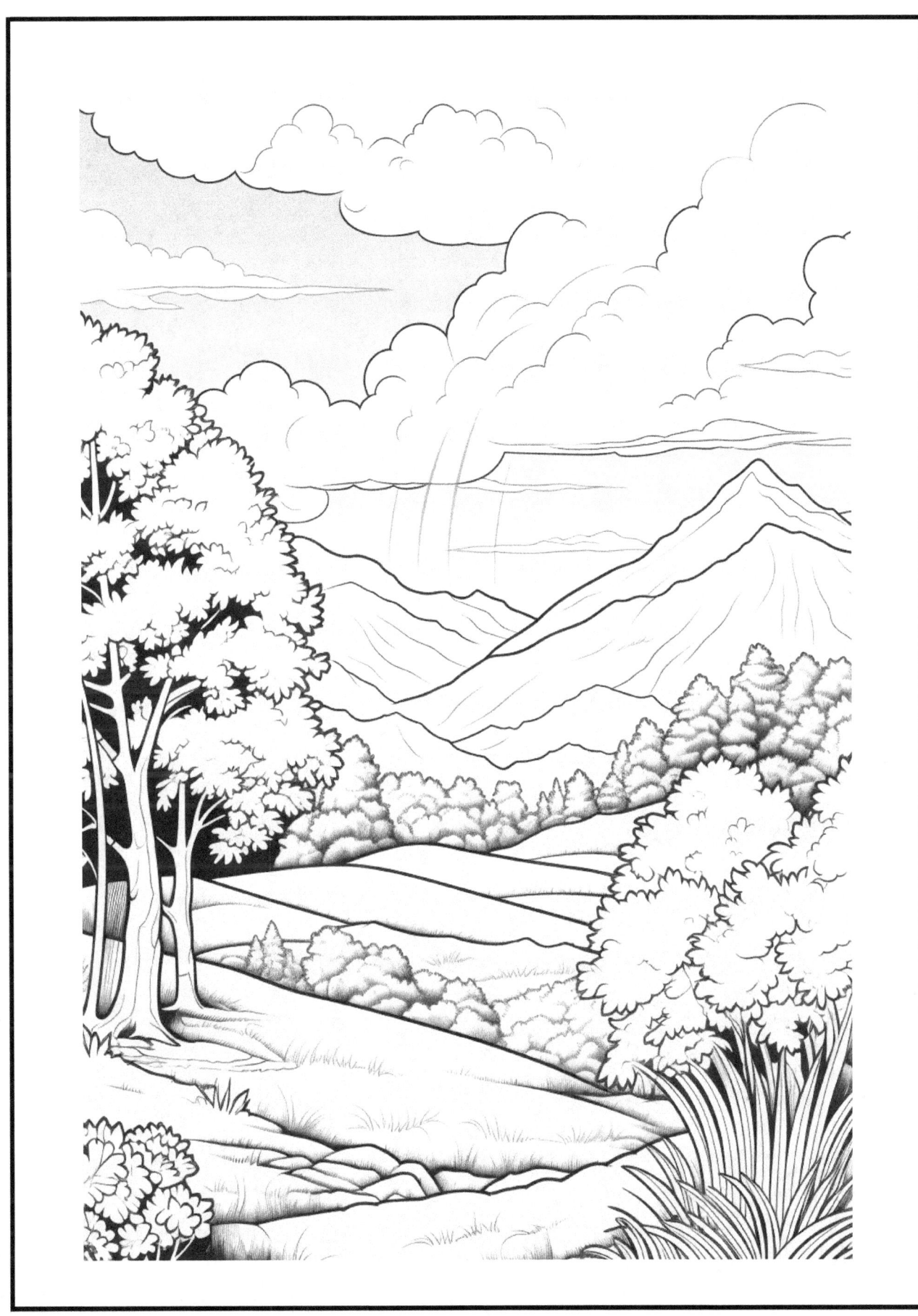

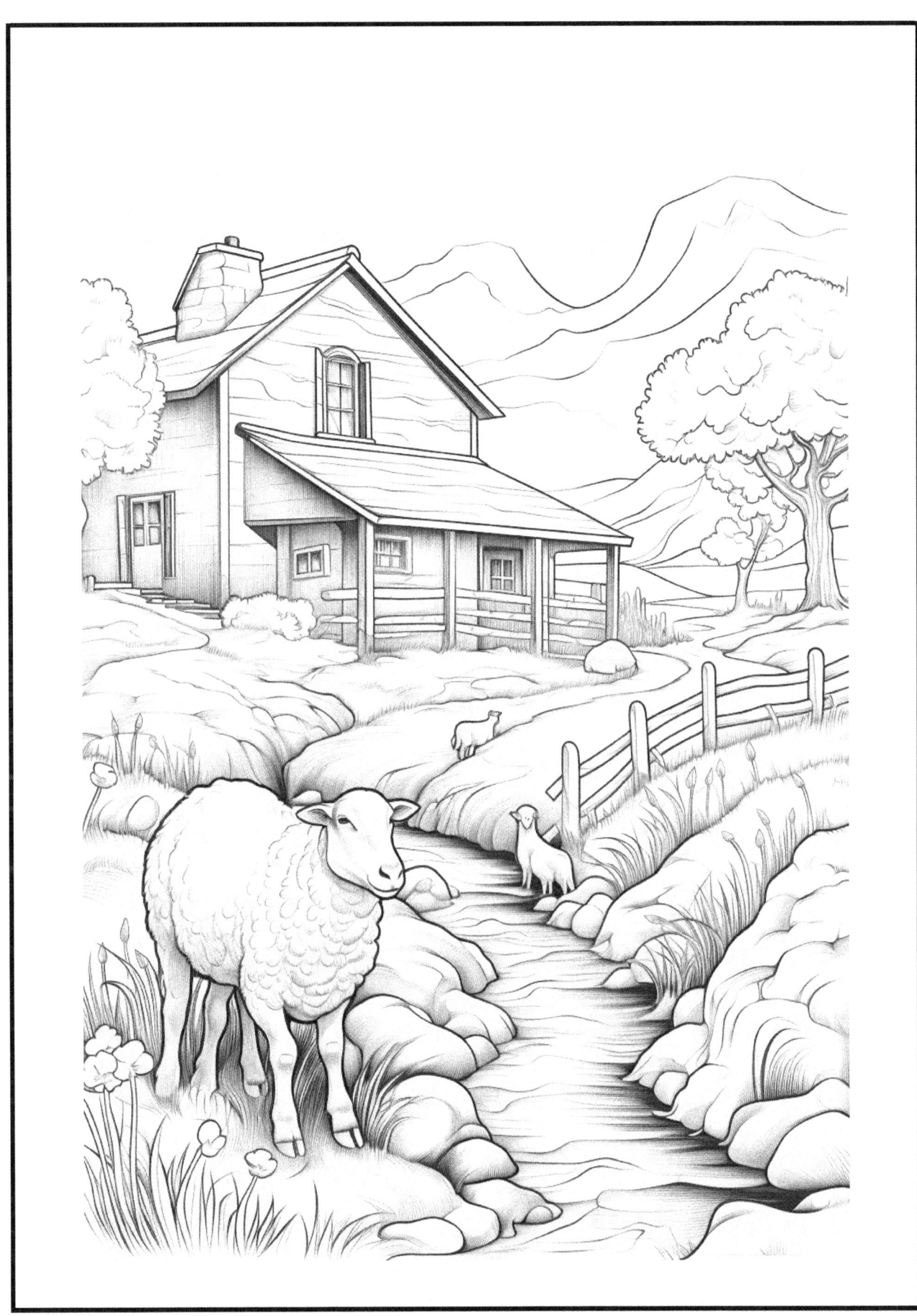

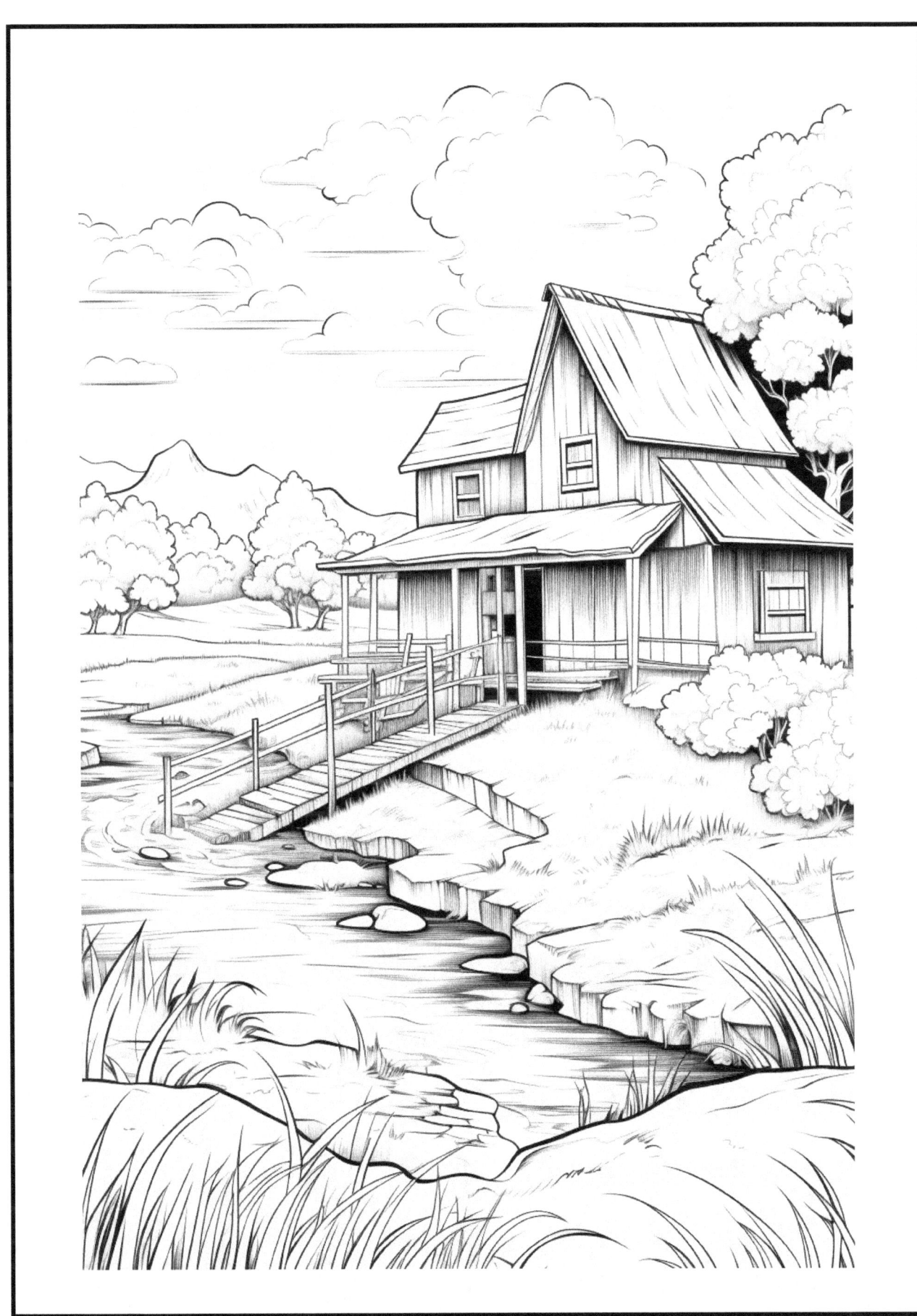

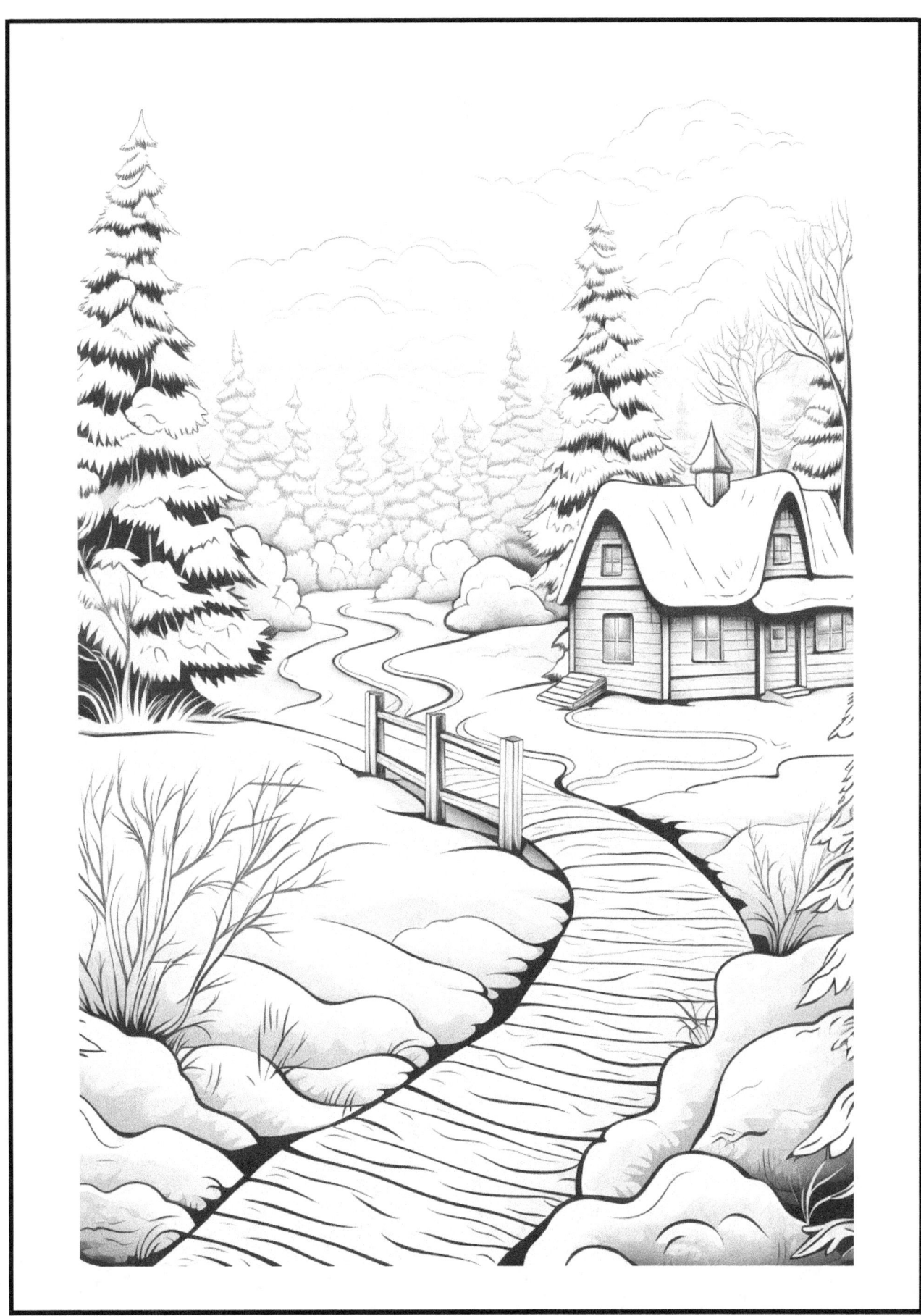

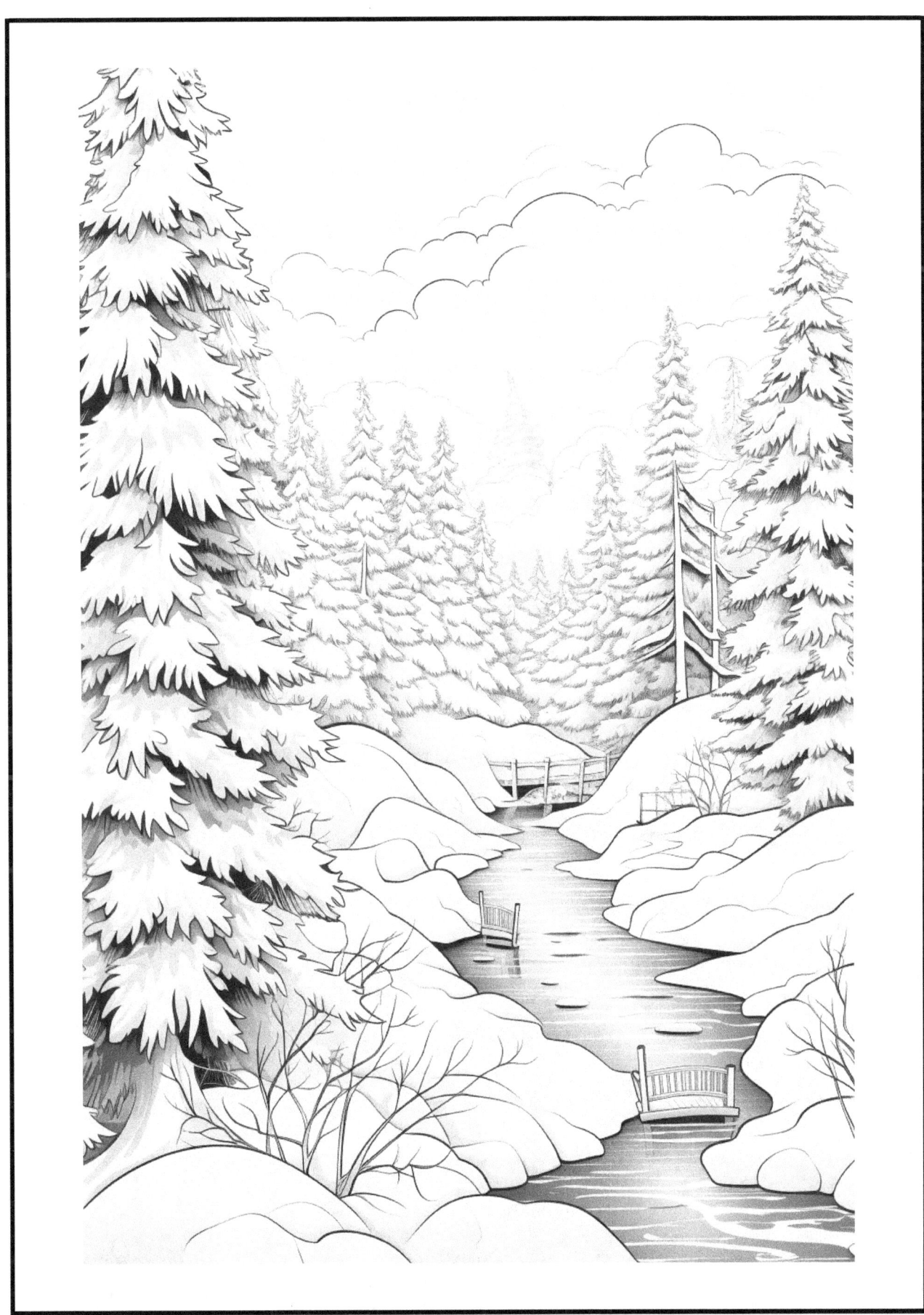

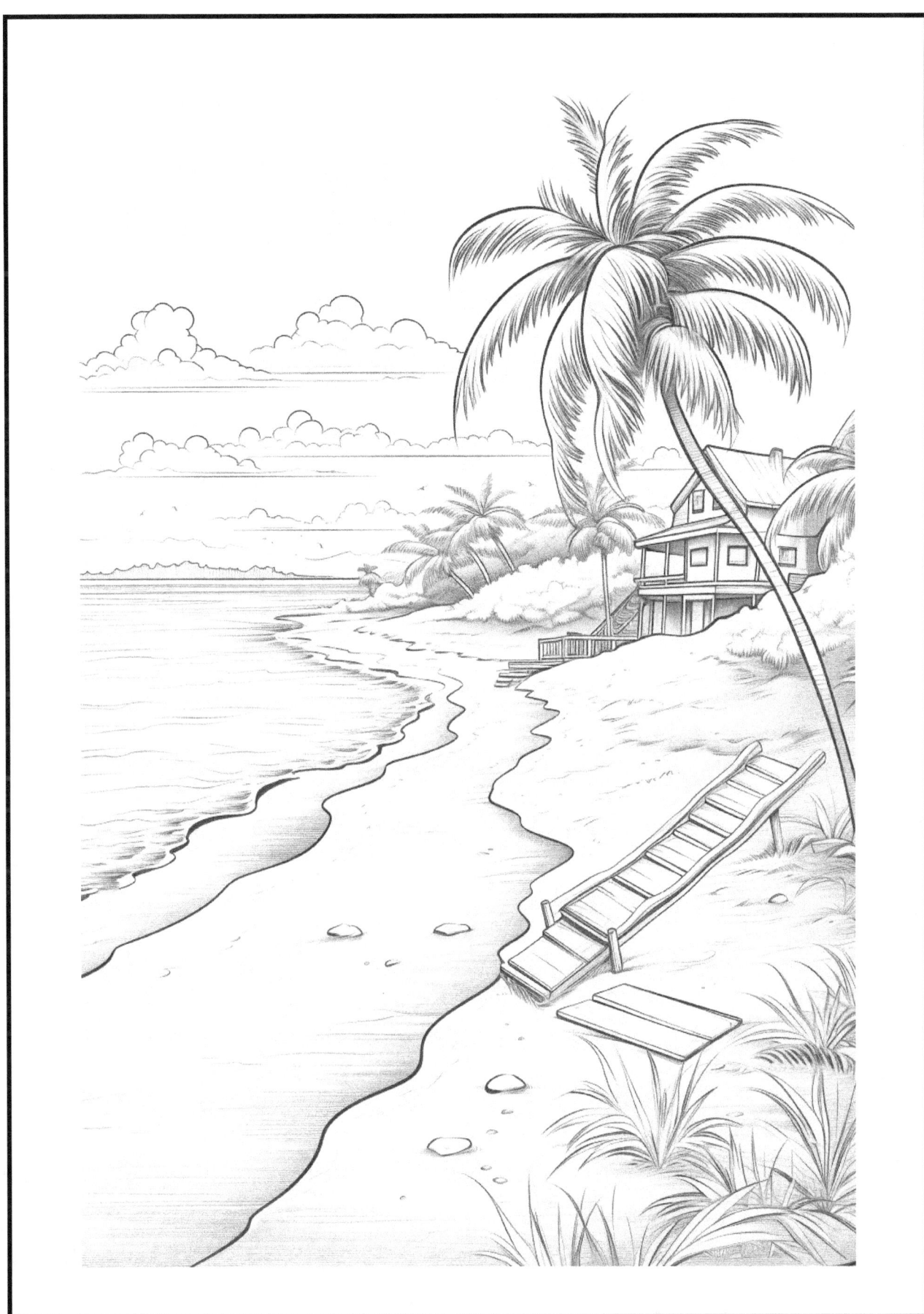

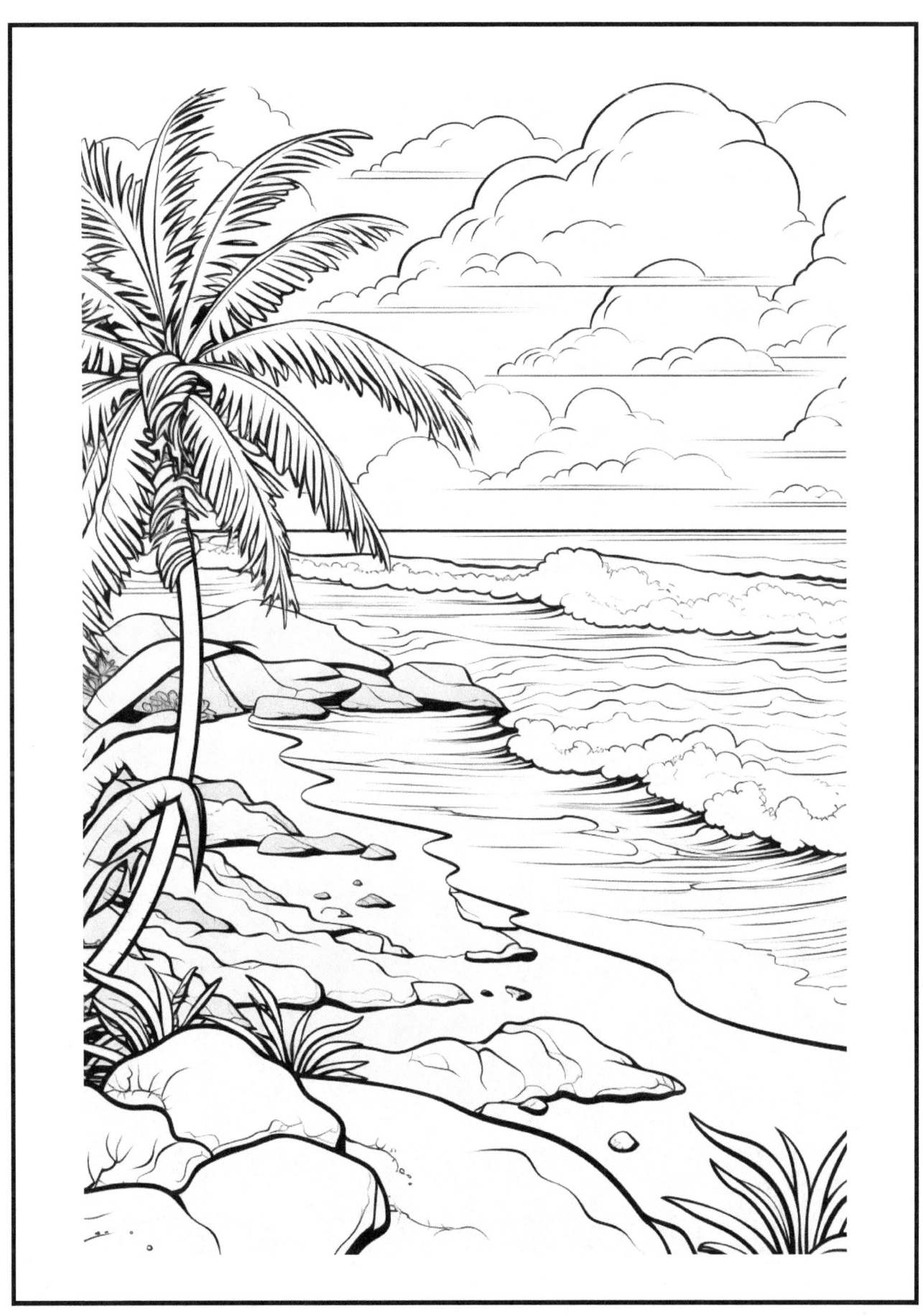

www.ingramcontent.com/pod-product-compliance
Lightning Source LLC
Chambersburg PA
CBHW082152290526

45794CB00008B/3263